THE PSALMS FOR TODAY

THE PSALMS FOR TODAY

By THOMAS COATES, 1910-

CONCORDIA PUBLISHING HOUSE
SAINT LOUIS, MISSOURI

To the memory of my father
THOMAS COATES, SR.

CONTENTS

FOREWORD

The meditations of this volume are devotional. That is to say, as the reader thinks each one of them through, he is drawn into communication with God and receives the stimulus for faith and life which God Himself has in store.

Devotional writing cannot be sentimental. It must traverse human joy and pain indeed; but it must help the reader confront God, who is greater than all our joys or pains.

Devotional writing must be Biblical. If it should bring God to the heart, it must speak as God speaks. This implies the honest attempt to say no more than God says; yet, in view of man's plight, also no less!

Devotional writing must take pains. It cannot be vagrant, slapdash. The best is none too good, in straightforward language, fitting phrase, apt figure, when words should bring God and man together.

In this volume Doctor Coates serves his readers with these hallmarks of devotional writing. His skill with language and his competence in interpretation of the Bible do not obtrude themselves.

The reader, I am sure, will be grateful for the opportunity to make his own contribution to these high devotional experiences — to read and reread them earnestly, prayerfully, joyfully.

RICHARD R. CAEMMERER

KEEPING GOD IN FIRST PLACE

From time to time it is important for each of us to rethink his goals and objectives. For what are we really striving in life?

The psalmist indicates the answer — the only correct answer: "I have set the Lord always before me." He is both the Guide along our way and the Goal at the end of our way. Our life will be satisfying and useful only if we live it in His service and to His glory. And our life will be well directed only if we focus our eyes on Him; with our spiritual sights trained on the heavenly goal, we shall not swerve from our course nor become bogged down in life's rutted byways. With the apostle, we must keep "looking unto Jesus, the Author and Finisher of our faith."

There is more to this matter of the well-directed life. God is not only *before* us, but He is also *beside* us — all the way. "He is at my right hand," says the psalmist. When we learned to drive an automobile, it was a comforting feeling to have an experienced driver sitting beside us, to keep our hand steady and our course straight and our actions right.

That is why we can share the assurance of the psalmist as we make our way through life: "Because He is at my right hand, I shall not be moved." When we try to "go it alone," sin blinds our eyes, confuses our mind, hobbles our steps. But He who has conquered sin enlightens our eyes, instructs our mind, directs our steps into the way of peace.

And so we see that all our life is related to God. When we "set Him before us," when we feel His strong and saving presence at our side, then we realize the full meaning of the apostle's words: "In Him we live and move and have our being."

That kind of life knows joy and peace. That kind of life has purpose and direction. That kind of life — already here and now — is eternal.

PSALM 45:2: *"Thou art fairer than the children of men; grace is poured into Thy lips."*

BEAUTIFUL SAVIOR

The story of Christian mission work really begins with the first appearance of the Savior to the Gentiles, the Magi who came from afar to worship at His crib. Because they saw Him, we Gentiles see Him, too. We see Him in the beauty of His grace. We call Him "Fairest Lord Jesus."

The psalmist, a thousand years before Jesus appeared, could give an accurate description of the Savior. He portrays Him as "fairer than the children of men." But the beauty which he discerns in Christ is spiritual rather than physical. Addressing our Lord, the psalmist says: "Grace is poured into Thy lips." That is poetry, to be sure — the poetry of salvation.

Many portraits of Christ have been painted. The artists all seek to bring out the nobility of His character, the beauty of His soul. But no picture can begin to do Him justice. His loveliness can never be captured on canvass. It is the loveliness of divine grace, the grace

3

which He personified and which He now imparts to men.

Each of us can paint a picture of our Savior — not with an artist's brush, but with the artistry of our daily lives. Is Christ "beautiful" in our lives? Does His glory shine through our words and actions? Or is our picture of Him only a sorry caricature? Sometimes we let Satan wield the paintbrush.

All Christendom enjoys the lovely hymn "Beautiful Savior, King of Creation, Son of God and Son of Man!" It is easy and pleasant to sing the words. It is somewhat more difficult to translate the words into life.

This is our spiritual task, this is our Christian witness: to enhance the Savior's beauty in the eyes of men by merging our lives with His and by letting His glory shine through.

PSALM 116:8: *"For Thou hast delivered my soul from death, mine eyes from tears, and my feet from falling."*

A THREEFOLD DELIVERANCE

"I walk in danger all the way," we sing in a moving hymn. But in the same hymn we go on to sing, "I walk with Jesus all the way." He is the Deliverer — the psalmist's and our own.

The first and greatest evil from which He delivers us is death. "Thou hast delivered my soul from death," the psalmist cries. This is the immortal Gospel theme: Christ triumphed over death. He delivered His own body from the grave and has promised the same to us. With the psalmist we can cling to the resurrection hope. Now death has lost its sting, and the grave has lost its dread. Life eternal is our heritage.

But more: Our Lord has delivered us from another evil. "Thou hast delivered . . . mine eyes from tears," the psalmist continues. This world has aptly been called a "vale of tears." Viewing the years of our earthly pilgrimage, Holy Writ declares, "Yet is their strength labor and sorrow."

We stagger at times beneath the load of our cares.

5

We are wounded sore by "the slings and arrows of outrageous fortune." Our eyes are consumed with tears as grief takes its heavy toll. We are brought at times to the brink of despair.

Just then it is that we need to heed the psalmist's words: "Thou hast delivered . . . mine eyes from tears." He is able to heal each aching wound. He is able to ease each heavy load. He is able to dry each scalding tear. For He it is who "hath borne our griefs and carried our sorrows."

Our Lord delivers us in yet a third way: "Thou hast delivered . . . my feet from falling." He rescues us from temptation. Earnestly, daily we must pray our Lord's own petition: "Lead us not into temptation." For daily the devil places stumbling blocks in our path, obstacles to make us trip, snares for our unwary feet.

But with our divine Protector at our side, we shall tread safely through the devil's maze and avoid the pitfalls of sin. He keeps our steps on the narrow way and guards our feet from falling. All through life He guides us with His counsel, and afterward He will lead us unto glory.

PSALM 19:1: *"The heavens declare the glory of God, and the firmament showeth His handiwork."*

THE HEAVENS ARE TELLING

The realm of creation testifies of God, testifies of His wisdom, His glory, His might. All nature is His temple. The stars, like a celestial choir, sing His praises. The stones preach of His power. The trees lift their arms to Him as in prayer. The hills and mountains tell of His strength. The lakes reflect His beauty. "The heavens declare the glory of God, and the firmament showeth His handiwork."

Where there is design, there must be a designer. Where there is a structure, there must be an architect. Where there is an effect, there must be a cause. All creation bears the imprint of the divine Creator.

With all this proof, so clear, so overwhelming, the bluster of the atheist sounds hollow indeed. "The fool hath said in his heart, There is no God." To reject the combined evidence of the universe is rankest folly. In the fullest sense of the word it is unnatural.

The glory of God fills the world. But there is a glory

7

that exceeds even that of creation. That is the glory of God's grace, revealed in Jesus Christ, His Son.

That glory is not always evident to men. God, in His own mysterious way, chose to hide it in strange forms. It shone forth from a manger. It welled from the lips of a twelve-year-old boy in the temple. It sparkled in the wine at Cana. It spoke quiet words to a fallen woman.

And that glory came to final focus on a cross. In Calvary's shame and anguish God's glory reached its height. The glory of God's grace appears in the symbol of man's sin.

And thus, as we daily thank God for the beauties of creation and as we listen raptly to what the heavens are telling, we thank Him still more for the beauties of grace and listen yet more intently to what the Gospel is telling.

We enjoy the glory of creation during our brief sojourn here. But we shall behold the glory of His grace eternally.

PSALM 63:3: *"Because Thy loving-kindness is better than life, my lips shall praise Thee."*

GRACE! 'TIS A CHARMING SOUND

"This is the life!" people are wont to say when their cup of joy is full, when they have their heart's desire, when their spirits are lifted high. The popular idea of "life" is pleasure, freedom from care. Life seems to be the highest good.

That is why people cling to life so desperately, seek always to improve it, wring the last ounce of enjoyment from it. To many, life is an end in itself. They look for nothing better, nothing beyond. They love it for itself.

But there is something better than life. The psalmist tells us what it is: "Thy loving-kindness is better than life." God is the Author and Source of all good. By His grace He enables us to share in that good. And that is better than life itself.

Our life on earth is, at best, short and full of woe. "We spend our years as a tale that is told." To build our hopes, our joys, and our ambitions on this life alone is to build on shifting sand.

God introduces us to a better life. It is not bound to this world or to this body. It is spiritual, eternal. It begins as soon as God's grace has entered and transformed our heart. "This is life eternal, that they might know Thee the only true God, and Jesus Christ, whom Thou hast sent," prayed our Lord.

To know and accept the loving-kindness of that God who has bestowed on us the gift of His own Son — that is life indeed. The life that is hid with Christ in God is better than what the world calls "life."

Because of God's surpassing grace in giving us the new life in Christ, the psalmist declares: "My lips shall praise Thee." Not just the lips, of course, but the whole heart will sing a continual paean of praise to God. Our lips will love to utter the charming sound of grace. Our ears will thrill to it. Our hearts will beat to it.

St. Augustine said it well: "O Lord, Thou hast formed us for Thyself, and our souls are restless till they rest in Thee."

But the psalmist said it better: "Thy loving-kindness is better than life."

PSALM 102:6: *"I am like a pelican of the wilderness; I am like an owl of the desert."*

THE PELICAN AND THE OWL

The psalmist was in dire straits. The woes of life engulfed him. His enemies plotted against him. His friends forsook him. His hopes were shattered. He knew no joy. The future was bleak. For him there were "fightings and fears within, without."

As he thought of his wretched state, he could compare himself only to the meanest of God's creatures. In his near despair he groaned: "I am like a pelican of the wilderness; I am like an owl of the desert." The comparison was apt. Both the pelican and the owl were unclean birds, according to the code which God had given His people. And both dwelt in solitude, unnoticed and unsought either by man or by their own kind.

We know full well how the psalmist felt. His very feelings have been ours. Like him, we have in effect classed ourselves at times with the pelican of the wilderness and with the owl of the desert.

For one thing, we have felt ourselves to be *unclean,*

11

stained and besmirched by sin. The sin that clings to our mortal frame. The sin that springs up in our heart. The sin of which we fain would rid ourselves, only to cry with St. Paul: "The good that I would, I do not; but the evil which I would not, that I do." The sin that drags us down, blunts our conscience, lures us on with its siren voice. The sin that leaves the taste of ashes in our mouth. The sin that makes us unclean — more unclean than even the pelican or the owl.

Then, too, we have felt ourselves to be *lonely* — unnoticed, unsought, unloved by men. Even, we tell ourselves in our despair, forgotten by God. With the psalmist we lament: "Hath God forgotten to be gracious? . . . Is His mercy clean gone forever?" And so we feel alone, solitary, forsaken, no better than the pelican of the wilderness or the owl of the desert.

But on both counts we are wrong. Unclean though we are by nature, and befouled by the presence of sin, the gracious promise of the Gospel is ours: "The blood of Jesus Christ, His Son, cleanseth us from all sin." We can wash our sin-stained robes and make them white in the blood of the Lamb. Through faith in Him we lose our guilty stains.

And, by the same token, we are not alone either. Men may forsake and forget us; the love of friends and brethren may grow cold. But God will hold us always in His everlasting arms. He says to us: "My presence shall go with thee, and I will give thee rest."

With Him at our side we are never alone. In His presence is fullness of joy.

PSALM 139:9-11: *"If I take the wings of the morning and dwell in the uttermost parts of the sea, even there shall Thy hand lead me, and Thy right hand shall hold me. If I say, Surely, the darkness shall cover me, even the night shall be light about me."*

THE WINGS OF THE MORNING

We are never alone. That indeed may be a disturbing thought. But to the Christian it is a comforting, reassuring thought.

The ever-watchful eye, the never-ending presence of God, is indeed a disturbance to the guilty conscience, to one who is involved in sin. The fact that even our wrongful thoughts are known to God is a sobering reminder. Indeed, it is meant to be.

The Christian, however, motivated by God's love and living in His Spirit, finds the abiding presence of God a source of comfort and strength. No matter where we go or what we do, our Lord is there with us. His help, His guidance, His protection never cease. "If I take the wings of the morning and dwell in the uttermost parts of the sea," as the psalmist puts it, the presence of God will be near.

His presence *guides* us. "Even there shall Thy hand lead me." Alone, our footsteps falter. Alone, we lose

13

the way. But when our Savior leads us, our goal is fixed and clear.

His presence *protects* us. "Thy right hand shall hold me." When the arms of God uphold us, then dangers lose their terror, and fear must take its flight.

His presence *gives us light.* "If I say, Surely the darkness shall cover me, even the night shall be light about me," the psalmist proclaims. At times despair and doubt enshroud us. A black pall of gloom envelops our spirit. The woes of life overwhelm us — we lose a loved one, a child brings us grief, our witness goes unheard, sickness enters our home, we cannot make ends meet. Then, with the psalmist we cry: "The darkness shall cover me!" Life seems dark indeed.

But then his further words ring clear: "Even the night shall be light about me." He is the Sun of our soul, of whom we can sing: "It is not night if Thou be near!"

And He is always near — even though we take the wings of the morning and dwell in the uttermost parts of the sea. He is always near — even amid the blackest night.

PSALM 119:71: *"It is good for me that I have been afflicted, that I might learn Thy statutes."*

THE BLESSINGS OF AFFLICTION

Down through the ages God's children have echoed the cry of Job: "Why must the righteous suffer?" It would be altogether proper and just, we are tempted to think, if the unbeliever or the worldling were to suffer misfortune, financial loss, a crippling accident, an early death. But — such is the seeming perversity of life — it is just the wicked who so often seem to prosper, who are the objects of fortune's smile.

The Christian, on the contrary, must often feel affliction's heavy hand. His way through life is hard; his woes multiply; his fond ambitions perish. Sometimes he is tempted to beat his fists against the wall and cry out, "Why?"

Such a reaction, to be sure, is natural for the flesh. The Christian is not immune to human emotions. But sometimes the devil uses those emotions to warp our judgment and relax our hold on God.

The Christian will rather confess with the psalmist: "It is good for me that I have been afflicted." Such a viewpoint is incredible to the unbeliever. Only the Christian can have this philosophy of life. For the believer sees behind every affliction the kind and loving hand of God. He knows that beyond the cross there waits the crown.

The psalmist knows why affliction strikes: "That I might learn Thy statutes." God does not spare the rod when He deals with His children. The pampered child becomes vain, selfish, proud. And so God would discipline His children, mold their character, and strengthen their will by sending them affliction.

Only thus do we learn God's statutes. Only thus do we bend our stubborn will to His kind and wise designs. Only thus do we blend our lives with Him.

For His statutes are always good. They are good for our life on earth. They alone show the way to goodness, love, and peace. And they are good for the life to come. They tell of Him who says: "I am the Way, the Truth, the Life; no man cometh unto the Father but by Me."

And so God would teach us His good and gracious will, not along the broad highway of pleasure, but rather down affliction's thorny path. But at the end of this road lies the shining goal of the mercy and love of God.

Till then His afflicted ones must walk in the faith that "all things work together for good to them that love God." That means that even our afflictions are good.

And why they are good we also know: That we may learn His statutes.

PSALM 42:7: *"Deep calleth unto deep at the noise of Thy waterspouts; all Thy waves and Thy billows are gone over me."*

GOD'S WATERSPOUTS

Life is often compared to a sea. The comparison is apt. The sea is sometimes calm, sometimes turbulent. So is life. The sea is dangerous and deep. Life is that way, too. The sea is uncharted; to cross it safely, we need a pilot, chart, and compass. That is true of life as well.

Like mariners on the deep, we are voyaging through life. The skies are clear, and the sea is serene. Then, suddenly, the gales begin to howl and the waves beat upon us, and we feel that we surely must sink.

Perhaps a crisis occurs in our personal life, and our plans for the future are upset. Perhaps there is trouble and conflict in the home. Perhaps a sickness overtakes us or one of our loved ones. Perhaps financial worries weigh us down. Perhaps we are criticized unjustly, our motives misconstrued. We are oppressed with a sense of failure.

The psalmist expressed well just how we have felt at such a time: "Deep calleth unto deep at the noise of

Thy waterspouts; all Thy waves and Thy billows have gone over me!"

How often we have felt that way when troubles have engulfed us! The waves are often so high that our heart fails us. We fear; we think surely that we shall sink and be drowned in the awful deep. We see no escape, and we cry in our despair: "All Thy waves and Thy billows are gone over me!"

But there is an escape. It lies in the mighty power of Him who is the "wondrous Sovereign of the sea." A word from His gracious lips will calm life's surging sea.

He speaks, and trouble's waves subside. He speaks, and the adverse winds grow still. He speaks, and the storm clouds pass away. He speaks, and we are afraid no more. He speaks, and we are safe at last. In the haven of His rest "there shall be no more sea."

To Him we cry as we steer our course through the waves and billows of life: "Jesus, Savior, pilot me, Over life's tempestuous sea!"

PSALM 77:13: *"Thy way, O God, is in the sanctuary; who is so great a God as our God?"*

WHERE GOD MAY BE FOUND

Man is by nature a worshiping creature. Man feels the innate need and impulse to worship, just as he feels the innate desire to eat or to sleep. By nature man knows that there is a Being higher than he, to whom he owes reverence and praise — and appeasement for his sins. In times of trouble and danger, even hardened unbelievers cry to God for help. It is the universal reaction of mankind to pray in times of need.

Unfortunately, however, ever since the Fall, man's knowledge of the true God has been distorted. Because of sin, man's impulse to worship has been perverted. His vision of the true God is beclouded. And so men by nature no longer know to whom they should pray, how they should worship, or what kind of sacrifices they should bring.

Men have, therefore, devised their own substitutes for the true God and conceived their own forms of worship and of sacrifice. Some make a graven image and put it in a shrine. Others profess to worship God in

19

nature, and to commune with Him in the cathedral of the great outdoors. To still others, God is simply a creative process or a philosophical idea, and with this God they would establish a harmonious relationship through positive thinking or moral living. Ultimately, all these conceptions of God have one common denominator: they are all projections of men's own ideas, and they all make salvation dependent upon man's own efforts. But in no such way can the true God be found.

The psalmist shows us the unerring way to God: "Thy way, O God, is in the sanctuary." In the place where His Word is proclaimed, in the place where His people meet, in the place set apart for His praise — here He would make Himself known.

Here, in the sanctuary, in the house of God, is His way — the way of His pardon, the way of His love, the way of His peace. Here in the sanctuary He makes His way into our hearts.

And here in the sanctuary we make our way to Him — to His cross, to His altar, to His Sacraments. Here in the sanctuary, in the assurance of His forgiveness and His fellowship, we commune with Him, our strong and present Lord, who is Himself the Way, the Truth, and the Life.

And we do not make our way to Him alone. For in the sanctuary we are joined with our fellow members of the body of Christ. This is the communion of saints, the unbroken circle of the redeemed, the universal family of God.

As we together find His way in the sanctuary, the psalmist's praise wells from our hearts: "Who is so great a God as our God?"

PSALM 89:47: *"Remember how short my time is."*

A SOBERING REMINDER

A group of young people, carefree and blithe, drive along the highway on a holiday outing; seemingly out of nowhere, a truck suddenly looms in their path, and there is death on the highway. A great airliner, laden with passengers, departs on a routine flight on a clear and sunny day; moments later it crashes into a mountainside, and death takes its heavy toll.

What shall we say when tragedy strikes and the candle of life is snuffed out? We instinctively echo the psalmist's warning: "Remember how short my time is." As we go through life, we are always but a step from the grave, but a heartbeat from eternity.

Medical science has made great strides in lengthening the average span of man's life. Scripture itself indicates that man may regard threescore years and ten as his life expectancy. And yet Holy Writ hastens to add: "And if by reason of strength they be fourscore years, yet is their strength labor and sorrow, for it is soon cut off, and we fly away."

Daily, therefore, we must remember how short our time is. It is utter folly to devote all our time and energy to the acquisition of earthly goods, as though we could possess them forever. It is equal folly to drain the cup of pleasure to its dregs, to escape the thought that all this must someday end. It is the part of wisdom — Christian wisdom — to remember how short our time is.

If we keep this sobering thought in mind, we shall live accordingly — not for the day, but for eternity; not for the things of the body, but for the welfare of the soul; not to gratify ourselves, but to "put on the Lord Jesus Christ."

If we remember how short our time is, then we shall always be ready for the moment when that time comes to an end. Daily we must ask ourselves: "Am I ready — *now* — if the Lord should summon me? Am I ready — *now* — to stand before His throne?" That is a sobering reminder indeed.

For the Christian, however, the reminder of life's brevity is a cause for joyous expectation. It is only this present life — so transitory, so vain — that will come to an end. It is only this mortal body — so weak, so frail — that will descend into the grave. Our soul is immortal, and our life is eternal, and our future is secure in the Paradise of God's love. That is the resurrection hope.

We must remember indeed how short our time is. But we must also remember how everlasting will be our life with Christ in God.

PSALM 27:5: *"For in the time of trouble He shall hide me in His pavilion; in the secret of His tabernacle shall He hide me; He shall set me up upon a rock."*

THE SAFE PAVILION

A traveler on a long and wearisome journey welcomes with glad relief the sheltering hostel in which he can find rest and refreshment. Such a haven becomes especially welcome when the storm begins to rage and the traveler's way grows difficult and dark.

For the pilgrim along life's tortuous way our God has provided a pavilion, a haven of safety and rest. This is no earthly shelter, no flimsy or perishable abode. This place of refuge is Himself, His love, His mercy, His protection.

That divine shelter means especially much to us when the winds of adversity beat upon us, when the gray clouds of worry and grief lower overhead and there is danger on the way that we must go. Then the psalmist's assurance can be ours: "In the time of trouble He shall hide me in His pavilion." That haven is warm with the glow of His love and bright with the light from the throne.

It is the way of the world to toss the casual remark: "Any port in a storm." But the Christian knows better. For him there is but one port in the storm of life — the safe pavilion of God's love.

But not everyone can find that place of safety and rest. It is known only to the children of God. They alone can find the way. That is why the psalmist declares: "In the secret of His tabernacle shall He hide me."

And just as the way to God's pavilion is known only to His redeemed, so also the peace and the comfort which there abides "none but His loved ones know." The secret of blessed communion with God is the sole possession, the unique heritage, of those who have traveled the way of the cross.

Travelers weary with the burden and heat of the day but made strong and glad by the promise of God will find eternal safety and peace. "He shall set me up upon a rock," the psalmist exults.

That is the rock of His forgiving, sustaining love. That rock shall never be moved. There He has pitched His pavilion. There we find rest on life's way.

MY TIMES ARE IN THY HAND

The pride and arrogance of unbelief has seldom been more clearly expressed than by the poet Henley in his famed poem "Invictus": "I am the master of my fate; I am the captain of my soul!" This is the boast of the man who has ruled God out of his life. This is the acme of his self-delusion.

Quite the contrary is the attitude of the Christian. He confesses: "God is the Master of my fate; He is the Captain of my soul." He makes his own the humble submission of the psalmist: "My times are in Thy hand."

This is an expression of Christian *trust*. There is no cause for worry about the future. The future belongs to God. All time is in His hand. He has dealt well with us in the past. He has withheld from us nothing that we needed for our spiritual or bodily wants. Can we not look with equal confidence to the future? On the basis of past performance, God has shown that He can be trusted. With full assurance we can say: "My times are in Thy hand."

25

Many persons, even in our enlightened and sophisticated age, look to fortunetellers for information as to the future or depend on astrology to guide their actions and decisions. This is but a modern refinement of "using witchcraft." It invites God's scorn and wrath.

We need not rely on the signs of the zodiac to plot our future course. We have a "more sure Word" — the unerring, unfailing wisdom of Him who all through life will "guide us with His counsel and afterward receive us to glory." Trusting Him, we say: "My times are in Thy hand."

This is also an expression of Christian *triumph*. Our future is not overshadowed by the fear of defeat or failure. We know that God will heed the prayer that we couch in the psalmist's words: "Deliver me from the hand of mine enemies and from them that persecute me."

It is not a pleasant thing to have enemies. But for the Christian it is inescapable, if he is true to his Christian convictions. It is still less pleasant to be persecuted. But that, too, is part of the Christian's lot, if he takes his faith seriously. All through life we are beset by the "old evil Foe" and by the malice of those who do his bidding.

But the powers of evil are already judged, already conquered. When we confess to God, "My times are in Thy hand," we glory in the fact that all the trials, woes, and fears that will arise to block our way to God have already been put to naught. The enemy's doom is sealed. "Weeping may endure for a night, but joy cometh in the morning."

How can we be sure? "My times are in Thy hand."

PSALM 87:5: *"And of Zion it shall be said, This and that man was born in her; and the Highest Himself shall establish her."*

THE NEW BIRTH IN CHRIST PREVIEWED

We haven't much to be proud of if we are really honest with ourselves. Even our best achievements are marred by imperfection; even our highest honors are transient. "All flesh is grass, and all the goodliness thereof is as the flower of the field," the prophet reflects. In future years our deeds will be forgotten and our name unknown.

There is one thing, however, of which we can justly be proud. We have one claim to fame that will never pass into oblivion. That is our high dignity as children of God, our status as citizens of His kingdom, as members of His church. That is a kind of honor by association.

The psalmist extols the church of God, which he calls by the poetic name "Zion." God Himself has established it. It is glorious because it reflects His glory. It is glorious because it brings its children to glory.

Into this sacred fellowship we have been born. We

27

can rejoice in that new spiritual birth, which is ours by His grace. We can point with pride to our spiritual birthplace. The psalmist is speaking of us when he testifies: "Of Zion it shall be said, This and that man was born in her." We are "this and that man."

All the credit for our new birth belongs to God. We are born into His family not by the will of man, but "by water and the Spirit." Our religious life and growth is not a process of raising ourselves by our own spiritual bootstraps. It rather means that we yield ourselves completely to the spirit of God, who is the Author of every good work, the Source of every pure desire.

New birth means new faith, new love, new hope, new life. Born anew, we have *faith* in Christ, whose atoning merits redeem us from our sin. Born anew we have *love* — love for God and our fellow men, which flows from His love for us. Born anew, we have *hope,* which enables us to look beyond the borders of time and to await the better joys of heaven. Born anew, we have *life* — life that is derived from God, that is directed toward God, and that finds its consummation in God.

That God has revealed Himself in His Son, Jesus Christ. He has established Zion, the communion of His saints. Into that elect fellowship we have been called.

This, and this only, is our glory: "Of Zion it shall be said, This and that man was born in her."

> Savior, since of Zion's city
> I through grace a member am,
> Let the world deride or pity,
> I will glory in Thy name.

PSALM 86:17: *"Show me a token for good, that they which hate me may see it and be ashamed; because Thou, Lord, hast holpen me and comforted me."*

A TOKEN FOR GOOD

The world at times seems to tumble down about our ears. Everything goes awry. We feel lonely, forsaken, misunderstood. Our hopes are unfulfilled. Our cherished projects fail. Friends disappoint us. Sorrows overwhelm us. The future is dark, uncertain, bleak.

Then, in our distress, we cry to the Lord: "Show me a token for good!" Any kind of token, Lord — if only it be good! Any kind of token, Lord, to show that You have not forgotten me!

The Lord has all manner of goodly tokens in reserve. At times they take on strange and unexpected forms. At times we do not immediately recognize them as good. At times, indeed, the Lord's tokens may seem downright evil.

But that is only in the light of our own poor, perverse judgment. We need always to remind ourselves that God moves in a mysterious way His wonders to

29

perform, and echo the poet's assurance: "Thy ways, O Lord, with wise design Are framed upon Thy throne above; And every dark and bending line Meets in the center of Thy love."

Our hearts are gladdened when the Lord shows us His tokens for good. They may be very simple — a friendly smile, an encouraging word, a welcome letter. Or they may be larger blessings: relief from bodily ills; a long-sought job for the family breadwinner; the salvaging of a marriage that seemed destined to fail; the safe return of a soldier boy; a reconciliation between estranged friends. Great or small, no goodly token is beyond the capacity of our Lord.

The best token of all, however, the Lord offers freely to everyone. That is the good token of salvation, procured for all men through the atoning sacrifice of Jesus Christ, His Son. He has shown us that token for good in His Word and Sacrament; that token is ours through faith.

Since He has shown us this best and greatest token, may we not be sure that He is both able and willing to show us the lesser tokens for good that we crave? "All that we need to support this body and life" — these tokens for good our Lord will not withhold from me.

His unfailing love for His people puts His foes to confusion. "That they which hate me may see it and be ashamed," cries the psalmist. The evils that surround us shall all be put to flight.

And thus, in the end, we shall echo the psalmist's song of praise: "Because Thou, Lord, hast holpen me and comforted me." In every need we have His help; in every sorrow we have His comfort. This is our present strength and our future hope.

PSALM 62:2, 3: *"He only is my Rock and my Salvation; He is my Defense; I shall not be greatly moved. How long will ye imagine mischief against a man? Ye shall be slain, all of you; as a bowing wall shall ye be and as a tottering fence."*

A BOWING WALL AND
A TOTTERING FENCE

Things do not always go smoothly in life for the Christian. At times the adversaries seem to get the upper hand. These adversaries are many, and they appear in different forms. Sometimes they are people; sometimes they are circumstances; sometimes they are the fear and the turmoil within our own heart and mind.

Against this array of malign foes the Christian must make his defense. But he cannot do this alone. He cannot stand unaided. He is too weak, too frail, too wavering. He is not even sure of himself. There are "fightings and fears, within, without."

But the strength and hope of the Christian life is that he need not stand alone. In time of adversity and strife he can find his defense in God — that God of whom the psalmist says: "He only is my Rock and my Salvation; He is my Defense."

31

With that divine defense he stands secure and safe. "I shall not be greatly moved," the psalmist exults. The slings and arrows of the foe may fly about him thick and fast. Sin and woe and death itself may batter at him cruelly. A thousand may fall at his side. But his confidence will not be shaken. He will win through in the end. He will not be greatly moved.

With this sublime assurance the man of God can taunt his evil foes: "How long will ye imagine mischief against a man?" The enemy's thoughts of victory will prove a delusion. He may even win some battles, but he will surely lose the war. And so the Christian can say to his foes: "Ye shall be slain, all of you." The final victory belongs to God — and to God's man.

And so the psalmist shows the futility of trying to oppose the will of God, of trying to defeat the man of God. To the adversaries he cries: "As a bowing wall ye shall be and as a tottering fence." Theirs is a hopeless cause.

By the same token the psalmist shows how needless, how wrong it is for the Christian to worry about the outcome of life's battles. Why should sorrow ever grieve him, why should troubles bring him low? His victory is already won, his triumph is already sure. For God, the mighty Captain, is forever on his side. And before the divine Victor even the mightiest foe is like a bowing wall and a tottering fence.

PSALM 30:5: *"For His anger endureth but a moment; in His favor is life; weeping may endure for a night, but joy cometh in the morning."*

TOMORROW WILL BE BETTER

"Hope springs eternal in the human breast," cries the poet. Thus he gives voice to the feeling, imbedded deeply in the heart of every man, that enables us to carry on, to see the goal ahead, to rise above despair. "There is always tomorrow," we say — and tomorrow will be better.

At times we feel the force of God's anger. That anger we have well deserved by our sin, our pride, our defiance of His will. That anger, to be sure, has been borne by Christ; He felt the full brunt of it on the cross. But the results of God's just anger over sin can be seen on every hand — in the wars and woes that beset our world; in the conflicts that rage within our breast.

God's anger, however hot, "endureth but a moment." It is His nature to love, rather than to be angry; not to punish, but to bless. And so "in His favor is life." That favor is ours through His grace; that life is ours through His Son.

33

Before we come to the eternal enjoyment of that life, however, we must do our share of weeping. This earth has well been called a "vale of tears." We weep when we think of our sins; we weep under the burden of care; we weep when we suffer life's sharp wounds, whether of body or of spirit; we weep as we stand by the grave; we weep together with our friends, for "often for each other flows the sympathizing tear." We need not be ashamed of our tears. Even Jesus wept.

But our weeping shall endure only "for a night." Of this the psalmist assures us: "Joy cometh in the morning." The night is long and the darkness deep, but the morning light will surely break.

Then it will be tomorrow. And tomorrow will be better. Tomorrow we'll be well again. Tomorrow we will find a job. Tomorrow our problem will be solved. Tomorrow the longed-for letter will come. Tomorrow our absent boy will return. Tomorrow our wound of today will be healed. Tomorrow holds our hope. Tomorrow we can sing. Tomorrow we shall live.

Yes, live — truly and fully — in the eternal tomorrow of God. In the warm and sure embrace of His love we shall find the true joy that cometh in the morning.

PSALM 114:1, 3, 4: *"When Israel went out of Egypt . . . the sea saw it and fled; Jordan was driven back. The mountains skipped like rams, and the little hills like lambs."*

THE SKIPPING HILLS

Time and again we have witnessed the power of God at work through the forces of nature. Wide areas of our country have been devastated by floods. Other sections have been shaken by earthquakes. Still others have been buffeted by gales. Indeed, "God plants His footsteps in the sea and rides upon the storm."

The powers of nature must do His bidding. But His bidding is never dictated by willfulness or caprice. His bidding is always the expression of His love and always the reflection of His concern for His people.

The Children of Israel learned that lesson early in their history. When they made their exodus from the land of Egypt and left their hateful bonds behind, all the powers of nature combined to aid them. First the Red Sea, then the River Jordan, parted their waters to give the Israelites safe passage. "The sea saw it and fled; Jordan was driven back," the psalmist recounts.

But more. When the voice of God thundered from the holy mount, Sinai quaked, and all the hills round-about trembled. Recalling the supernatural earthquake, the psalmist cries: "The mountains skipped like rams, and the little hills like lambs."

That is poetry, of course. But in a vivid and graphic way it shows how the realm of nature must yield to the voice of God and how His mighty hand controls the elements like puppets on a string.

And the beneficiaries of God's action in nature are His people, the objects of His love and care and of His redemption through the merits of Jesus Christ. This fact may at times be difficult to grasp, when the flood waters rush, the hurricane blows, and the earth beneath us quakes — when, as the psalmist puts it, the hills begin to skip.

But our life is built on a firmer foundation than even Gibraltar itself. That foundation is the Word and promise of God. Built on this eternal rock, we never shall be moved. Built on this eternal rock, the floods may rage and the hills may skip, but our house will stand secure. Built on this eternal rock, we know that "every dark and bending line meets in the center of His love."

PSALM 61:2: *"From the end of the earth will I cry unto Thee when my heart is overwhelmed; lead me to the rock that is higher than I."*

THE ROCK THAT IS HIGHER THAN I

Hamlet was overwhelmed. Obsessed by feelings of frustration, perplexed by the mysteries of life, he knew no place of recourse. Suicide appeared at times to be the best solution to his dilemma. He soliloquized: "To be or not to be, that is the question," and he debated the alternatives: "Whether 'tis nobler in the mind to suffer the slings and arrows of outrageous fortune, or to take arms against a sea of troubles and, by opposing, end them."

We, too, at times are overwhelmed. We are engulfed by the rising, inexorable flood of trouble. We cannot stem the surging tide of woe. In our distress we echo the psalmist's plaintive cry: "All Thy waves and Thy billows are gone over me."

Unlike Hamlet, however, the Christian is not driven to despair. When the waves loom high and the billows roar, he does not yield to hysterical frenzy. Nor does he fold his arms in stoical resignation, indifferent to his fate.

When the Christian's heart is overwhelmed, his voice breaks its silence. He cries to God — the God who is ready to hear and eager to help. He cries to God, no matter how low he may have sunk or how far he may have been driven — even "from the end of the earth."

And his cry is not of despair but of trust: "Lead me to the rock that is higher than I." Nearly drowned beneath the whelming flood, the Christian clutches the rock. God has placed the rock there for just that purpose. He wants us to cling to it. He wants it to save us from the flood.

The rock is "higher than I." That is why we can trust it. The waves lash against it in fury, but it stands unmoved and strong. The rolling tides of the ages beat upon it in vain. It is high enough and strong enough to offer a hold to every clutching hand.

The rock is Christ. He is higher than we, as heaven is higher than earth, as God is higher than man. Because He is higher, He is holier. Because He is higher, He is stronger.

Clinging to that rock, we are safe from the whirlpool of sin, from the crashing waves of trouble. That rock looms high over the perils of the sea.

PSALM 141:3: *"Set a watch, O Lord,
before my mouth; keep the door of my
lips."*

GUARD MY LIPS!

During World War II, signs were
posted with the warning: "Careless talk costs lives!"
There is indeed no way of estimating how much dam-
age — physical, mental, and spiritual — has been
caused by careless talk. No wonder St. James calls the
tongue "a fire, a world of iniquity . . . an unruly evil,
full of deadly poison." Strong words, but only too true!

Every one of us, therefore, must echo the psalmist's
prayer: "Set a watch, O Lord, before my mouth; keep
the door of my lips." We need God's answer to this
prayer, for our own sake and for the sake of others.

For ourselves we need "a watch before our mouth"
in order to preserve the consistency of our faith, the
sincerity of our worship. It is unthinkable, declares
St. James, that out of the same mouth both blessing
and cursing should proceed. The mind that is purified
with the love of Christ will not produce vulgarity, pro-
fanity, or falsehood. The heart in which the Holy Spirit
dwells will not be the source of malicious gossip.

39

Evil words come from the Evil One. The very name "devil" means "slanderer." He tempts us to slander God by taking the holy name in vain. He tempts us to slander our neighbor with cruel and cutting words. A loose tongue betokens a loose faith. Earnestly we must pray, "Keep the door of my lips!"

We need this spiritual safeguard also for the sake of others. Careless, profane, impure words, when uttered by a Christian, cause offense. They lead others to doubt the genuineness of our faith. They bring the church into disrepute. They cast a shadow on the Gospel's light. Others can judge us only by how we talk and by how we act. The example that we set is the basis for their judgment. What kind of example do we show?

Daily we must pray, "Set a watch, O Lord, before my mouth; keep the door of my lips." Thus guarded and secure, our mouth will show forth His praise, and our lips will be opened to tell the wonders of His love.

That love He has revealed in Christ, whose lips were full of grace and in whose mouth was found no guile.

PSALM 4:8: *"I will both lay me down in peace and sleep; for Thou, Lord, only makest me dwell in safety."*

SAFE IN THE LORD

Some people of our acquaintance moved away from the city because they thought it would be a likely target for an enemy bombing raid. They moved to the country to be "safe."

There is a better place of safety — the arms of the Lord. With the psalmist we can declare: "Thou, Lord, only makest me dwell in safety." Enclosed in His strong embrace, we cannot be touched by any ill. He sends His angels to guard our steps, to ward off the lurking perils of our path. In Him we are calm and safe as we tread the unknown way.

He has defeated the archenemy of our souls. "He can harm us none; he's judged, the deed is done." Shall the God who was strong enough to destroy the gates of hell be too weak to stay the impact of a bomb? Only the unbelievers quake with fear. God's children dwell in safety. Waking or sleeping, we are His.

The psalmist, then, can have the confidence to say: "I will both lay me down in peace and sleep." No haunt-

41

ing fear need mar the Christian's slumber. He need not dread the dawn. He lies down with trust, sleeps in peace, and awakes refreshed — because in the Lord he feels safe.

At exactly 12:05 every Monday afternoon, in our city, the air-raid siren wails. It is part of our "civil defense" program. It is an eerie sound, enough to chill the blood. For the Christian, though, it holds no threat — not even if the danger were real. The Christian hears a stronger voice and a sweeter sound: "Be not afraid, neither be thou dismayed; for the Lord, thy God, is with thee whithersoever thou goest."

Luther said it well: "He defends me against all danger and guards and protects me from all evil." But the psalmist said it still better: "Thou, Lord, only makest me dwell in safety."

In Him we are safe — by day and night, on land and sea, in youth and age, in body and soul, in life and death, in time and eternity.

PSALM 49:17: *"For when he dieth, he shall carry nothing away; his glory shall not descend after him."*

"YOU CAN'T TAKE IT WITH YOU!"

Some years ago a stage play entitled "You Can't Take It with You" received much popular acclaim. The theme struck a responsive chord; in blunt words it expressed a philosophy to which most people readily subscribe. No matter how much wealth or property or fame or power a man may amass, he cannot take it with him into the hereafter. Man's earthly fortunes are bounded by the grave.

Even though this fact appears to be obvious, a great many people give the impression — by their greed for gain, their lust for power, their vaulting ambition — that they actually *can* "take it with them." Down through history men have been animated by a mad lust for gold. For the sake of gold they have lied and stolen and killed. The desire for gold has been the burning obsession of their lives — more important to them than honor, family, friends — or God. In fact, gold — or its material equivalent — has become their god.

Our Lord told a parable about a man like that. He wanted to show the folly of a man who "layeth up treasure for himself, and is not rich toward God." To such a man, sooner or later, the harsh, inexorable summons will come: "Thou fool, this night thy soul shall be required of thee." And then follows the inevitable question: "Then whose shall those things be, which thou hast provided?" Riches, houses, goods — all must be left behind. "You can't take it with you!" we say. The psalmist says it more solemnly: "For when he dieth, he shall carry nothing away."

This applies not merely to wealth, however. It applies with equal force to man's craving for power, prestige, "the pride of life." We are reminded of this fact in every political campaign. The stakes are high: fame, power, national prominence, the opportunity to shape the affairs of men and of the nation. But this, too, is fleeting, transient. Man's place in the sun lasts but for a little day. "His glory shall not descend after him," avers the psalmist.

There is but one thing that we can take with us beyond the grave. That is the treasure of salvation, wrought for us by Christ and bestowed on us through His Spirit. This treasure neither moth nor rust can corrupt, nor can thieves break through and steal it. This treasure, "laid up" in heaven, is our only enduring prize. It must be the sole object of our love, our hope, our ambition.

For where our treasure is, there will our heart be also.

PSALM 119:83: *"For I am become like a bottle in the smoke; yet do I not forget Thy statutes."*

A BOTTLE IN THE SMOKE

We feel at times as though the world has passed us by. We feel forsaken, neglected, discarded. Worn with toil, weakened by affliction, forgotten by our friends, we seem to have outlived our usefulness. We can no longer summon our former strength, our former zest, our former love.

This is how David felt when he wrote this psalm. He described his feelings with a vivid picture: "I am become like a bottle in the smoke." A leather bottle, hanging for a long while in the smoke, not only became blackened with soot; it became dried, parched, and shriveled up.

Who wants a bottle like that? Of what further use is it? Who will put wine into such a bottle? It is good only to be cast aside.

David felt like such a bottle in the smoke. He was old and sick and weary. He was no longer the robust hero, the sweet singer, the regal monarch. The tide of life had turned. Or so he thought.

45

Sometimes we, too, feel like "a bottle in the smoke." Weary, disillusioned, oppressed with a sense of failure, we feel as though we were fit only for the discard. Despair holds us in its grip.

At times there may be good cause for us to feel like David. But more often we are not actually like "a bottle in the smoke." We only think we are. Have we a really good reason to droop and be melancholy? Have we really been slighted and neglected as grievously as we suppose? Or is it just our imagination playing us false?

At such a time we must, with the Spirit's help, listen to David's reminder: "Yet do I not forget Thy statutes." No matter how low our spirits sink, our God can always lift us up. No matter how far from Him we stray, His love would always call us back.

His statutes are gentle to hear and strong to save. Listen to them now: "They that wait upon the Lord shall renew their strength; they shall mount up with wings as eagles; they shall run and not be weary; and they shall walk and not faint."

If we remember God's statutes, we shall not feel like "a bottle in the smoke." We shall not feel forsaken, for He is near. We shall not feel unloved, for He loves us still. We shall not become weary, for He gives us strength.

A bottle in the smoke? No, rather, "a burning and a shining light."

PSALM 68:18: *"Thou hast ascended on high, Thou hast led captivity captive. Thou hast received gifts for men."*

THE DIVINE CAPTOR

Satan is a prisoner of war. The evil Foe of human souls, who held mankind captive in the bonds of sin, has himself been captured. The Despoiler of men has met his match in the Redeemer of men.

Now the Son of God returns home to show His Father the trophy. "The strife is o'er, the battle done; Now is the Victor's triumph won." It is V-Day in the kingdom of God.

David in prophecy sang of the Lord's ascension: "Thou hast ascended on high, Thou hast led captivity captive." For forty days after His glorious resurrection the Lord Jesus remained among His disciples. By many infallible proofs He showed them — and all mankind — that He had truly risen from the dead. He tarried with them long enough to convince them that their hope was not in vain, that their faith was firmly grounded. Henceforth they could testify for their risen Lord as eyewitnesses of His glory.

47

Now He needed to tarry no longer. It was time for Him to return home. His Father awaited Him. The holy angels were ready to welcome Him.

And so, as the disciples, clustered on the hilltop, gazed in reverent awe, He was taken up, and a cloud received Him out of their sight. They could make the psalmist's words their own: "Thou hast ascended on high!"

But more. They could exclaim in triumph, "Thou hast led captivity captive!" The chains of death are broken. The bonds of sin are severed. In the battle for the souls of men the tables are forever turned.

What does this mean to us? "Thou hast received gifts for men," the psalmist sings. Jesus returned to the realms of glory, there to send down to us the endless stream of His gifts. And what gifts they are! All that we need to supply our body; all that we need to nourish our soul.

And above all, the gift of freedom. The ascended Lord has freed us forever from the hateful manacles of sin. We now enjoy "the glorious liberty of the children of God." That freedom is more than a word. That freedom is the key to life.

Free! Ah, yes, but free only because we are caught in the toils of a new and holier bondage. Our captor is the Son of God. We are held in the fetters of His love. We are bound to Him by faith. It is strange, but true: In that bondage alone we are free.

O Lord, who hast led captivity captive, bind us to Thee with the cords of Thy love!

PSALM 46:9: *"He maketh wars to cease unto the end of the earth."*

NO MORE WAR

War is the ultimate tragedy of the human race. It either embodies or gives rise to the whole catalog of the evils and miseries known to man. In our own day much of the good earth that God created has been reduced to ruin. Upon its shambles the spirits of hell have held high carnival.

But the foul vapors of war are dispelled by a ringing voice: "He maketh wars to cease unto the end of the earth." Without God's blessing, all the international conferences and alliances, all the covenants and treaties for the preservation of peace, are foredoomed to failure.

It is God alone who can establish and maintain peace "unto the end of the earth." Both war and peace serve His eternal purposes. Even the dread war god becomes the executor of the divine will.

Since war is a product of sin, we cannot expect a warless world until we have a sinless world. That, we know, will not happen this side of Judgment Day. That

49

fact, however, does not excuse us as Christians from our responsibility to work for a lasting peace.

As Americans celebrate their national Independence Day, the concern for a just and lasting peace is uppermost in their minds. The thought of another war strikes horror to the soul. Our daily prayer must be that God would avert this calamity from us.

And yet, preparations for war go on apace. Jet bombers, air-raid sirens, civil defense warnings, huge expenditures for arms — all these bear eloquent witness to the fact that the peace that we enjoy is uneasy and unsure.

As we view all this, the words of the ancient litany spring to our lips: "From war and pestilence . . . good Lord, deliver us!" Independence Day reminds us with redoubled force that our constant task must be to "seek the peace of the city." That task must be sanctified by prayer.

To pray for peace, to use our influence for peace, and to exemplify peace in our life and relationships — this is our peculiar work and responsibility as Christian citizens. We must align ourselves with Him and bring others to know Him, who alone can "make wars to cease unto the end of the earth."

That, beyond doubt, is the Christian's great and unique contribution to the peace of the nation and of the world.

PSALM 126:1-3: *"When the Lord turned again the captivity of Zion, we were like them that dream. Then was our mouth filled with laughter and our tongue with singing; then said they among the heathen, The Lord hath done great things for them. The Lord hath done great things for us; whereof we are glad."*

IT SEEMS LIKE A DREAM

Dreams at times can be pleasant things. Our fondest ambition is realized, a delightful experience is ours, a happy reunion occurs — and then we awaken. "It was only a dream," we lament, as we turn to the grim realities of life.

Sometimes our dreams come true. Sometimes our fondest ambition *is* realized, sometimes incredible happiness *is* ours, sometimes a longed-for reunion *does* occur. Then we are apt to exclaim, "Why, it seems like a dream!"

The psalmist tells how Israel's dream came true. For seventy years God's people had languished in hateful exile, yearning for their homeland, weeping for their loved ones, grieving for their temple, now in ruins.

Then their fortunes turned, and they could go home. Their happiness knew no bounds. "Then was our mouth filled with laughter and our tongue with singing," the psalmist cries. It seemed too good to be true. "We were like them that dream," he recalls.

51

Even the heathen were impressed. As they observed the joy of God's people, their hopes fulfilled and their homes restored, these neighbors marveled: "The Lord hath done great things for them!"

We, too, have seen our dreams come true. Not at the foot of the rainbow, to be sure, but at the foot of the cross. There we find forgiveness, full and free. There we reclaim our lost inheritance — a place in the family of God. There we blend our life with His.

And thus we can echo the psalmist's praise: "The Lord hath done great things for us." Ours is no mere release from human exile, but from the bondage of sin. Ours is no mere return to an earthly homeland, but to the heavenly Canaan. Ours is no mere transient joy, but the glad hosannas of the ransomed saints before the throne of God.

And the Lord, who has done such great things for us in terms of our spiritual blessings, shall He not also provide for our every need of body and life? He who has done the greater will also provide for the lesser.

It may seem like a dream, but it is divinely, eternally true.

THE NOISE OF MANY WATERS

Those who live near the sea are used to the pounding of the surf. To those who are unaccustomed to the roar, it has a strange and ominous sound.

The sea inspires men with dread. For ages on end the waves keep breaking on the rock-bound coast. The deep has claimed many a human life. In its waves many a ship has foundered. The tempests lash the waters into a foaming, seething fury. The noise of many waters causes many a human heart to quake.

We are all voyagers on the sea of life. That sea is not always calm. The frail bark of our life is often tossed by adversity's waves. The sky is often overcast with the clouds of worry and doubt. Sometimes, it seems, we lose the mariner's compass. We drift aimlessly, far off our charted course. We know the perils of the deep. The noise of many waters keeps pounding in our ears — the waters of sin and sorrow and death. We wonder: Shall we ever reach the shore?

53

But the sea, for all its dreadful power, for all its deafening roar, has its Master. His voice can bid the waves subside. His voice can calm the troubled deep. His voice can still the tempest's roar.

"The Lord on high is mightier than the noise of many waters." With this Pilot at the helm, our bark will steer a steady course. He knows how to clear the treacherous shoals. He guides us safely to the shore.

It is good to feel our Pilot near as we sail life's stormy sea. It is good to know that the mighty waves must yield to their mightier Lord. It is good to have His shelter from the lashing of the gales.

On the eternal shore of His love and grace, there is safety and peace and rest. This is the calm and happy haven for all the redeemed of God.

GLORIOUS THINGS OF THEE ARE SPOKEN

"Zion" — a poetical term for the city of Jerusalem — is one of the titles which the Bible ascribes to the Holy Christian Church. The church is the "city of God." It is the place which He has chosen for His habitation and in which His Spirit dwells.

Augustine, the great church father, wrote a classic treatise on "The City of God." In it he showed that, although the earthly city — the kingdom of this world — should perish, the heavenly city will forever endure. Against the Holy Christian Church even the gates of hell shall not prevail.

Of this "city," says the psalmist, "glorious things are spoken." This city is glorious because of its divine Founder, the Son of God Himself. It is glorious because the glad bells of peace ring out within its borders — peace between God and man. It is glorious because it has been made white and clean by the blood of Jesus

Christ. It is glorious because its citizens are heirs of eternal glory.

To dwell in the city of God is life's highest privilege. We Christians are citizens of no mean city; we belong to the commonwealth of the elect. When Satan and his hosts besiege the holy city, as they do constantly, we must watch its ramparts and keep its banner flying.

We should be careful, too, not to stray outside its walls. Anywhere beyond the borders of God's city is "off limits" for the Christian. Only in Zion's strong enclosure is there safety for our souls.

In the city of God there is no ghetto. There are no restrictive covenants to separate one group from another. For in the community of the redeemed there are no second-class citizens. Here there is no distinction of race or color or social status. Here "brother clasps the hand of brother" in the perfect equality of the children of God. For in Christ Jesus all are one.

The task of extending the borders of God's city and of building its walls never stops. That is the perennial, endless work of Christian missions. In that work we all must share.

It was said of Sir Christopher Wren, the builder of St. Paul's Cathedral, that he had a "fever for building." We should have a fever for building the walls of Zion. That fever should spread from us, as we go through life, like a holy contagion.

> Savior, since of Zion's city
> I by grace a member am,
> Let the world deride or pity,
> I will glory in Thy name.

PSALM 57:1: *"Be merciful unto me, O God, be merciful unto me, for my soul trusteth in Thee; yea, in the shadow of Thy wings will I make my refuge, until these calamities be overpast."*

WHEN CALAMITY STRIKES

These words are familiar to every penitent, trustful soul. They reflect human experience, and they speak to human need. Often we are oppressed by the calamitous nature of our sin and our weakness. Often we must fly for refuge to the shadow of God's wings.

The psalmist bewailed "these calamities." God's hand lay heavy upon him. His life was in danger. The future was dark.

Calamity sometimes strikes us, too. A father is cut down in the prime of life, leaving a widow and children bereft. The fury of nature is unleashed, with thousands homeless and destitute in its wake. There is a sickening crash on the highway, and promising lives are snuffed out.

When calamity strikes at our life, our first impulse is to yield to blind despair. The future seems blank. All hope has fled.

But the Christian knows better than to despair.

57

In his distress he turns instinctively to God as David did, and cries: "Be merciful unto me, O God, be merciful unto me!" In the wideness of God's mercy there is balm for every wound. In the arms of His compassion there is rest for weary souls. In His all-pervading goodness we can place our dearest trust.

The psalmist said it thus: "Yea, in the shadow of Thy wings will I make my refuge, until these calamities be overpast." The picture is lovely and apt. Like a mother bird who spreads her wings to shelter her young from the stormy blast or from the lurking foe, so God envelops His children in the protecting folds of His love. In that place of refuge no evil can befall us, no foe can do us harm.

There we shall abide "until these calamities be overpast." The perils and woes of this life, calamitous as they may seem, will all pass away. Sin will lose its power, and death will lose its sting. These things do not abide.

But God abides, now and evermore. In His protection we are kept safe. In His salvation we are made free.

PSALM 76:6, 7: *"For promotion cometh neither from the east nor from the west nor from the south. But God is the Judge; He putteth down one and setteth up another."*

TRUE PROMOTION AND ADVANCEMENT

It is natural to be ambitious, to want to "get ahead." We have a rather poor opinion of people who have no ambition. They are shiftless, we say. They lack an important ingredient of human behavior.

At graduation time our thoughts are especially focused on the matter of advancement, of human progress. School children expect to be "promoted." High school graduates come to a fork in the road and are faced with the alternatives of going to college, getting a job, or entering military service. College graduates stand on the threshold of their life's career, with new worlds to conquer. For all of these there is no such thing as standing still. If they are normal, they feel the inner drive to climb higher, to go forward.

Men and women in business and in the professions, too, desire advancement if they are worth their salt. Such advancement may appear in various forms: new opportunities for service, greater responsibility, a higher position, a better salary. It is natural to want to "be promoted."

It is natural, to be sure, but is it Christian? That depends on the motivation that gives rise to the desire. Ambition is a noble thing when it is properly motivated and rightly directed. To be ambitious, in the Christian sense, means nothing else than to exercise good stewardship — of our abilities, our opportunities, our time.

But ambition that is wrongly motivated and misdirected is a frightening, tragic thing. The path of history is littered with the bones of tyrants whose ambition has proved their undoing. The daily paper tells many a pathetic tale of people who have been overly ambitious — for the wrong things, in the wrong way. They have sought "promotion," as the psalmist indicates, from the west or east or south. That is, they have fixed their attention on things below. They have looked for advancement from human sources and for selfish reasons. Their ambition has "gone to their head."

Ambition, however, is good only if it "goes to our heart." True promotion comes not from below but from above. "God is the Judge," says the psalmist. He knows why we want to "get ahead." If our motives are right, He will enable us to "get ahead." It all depends on Him.

"He putteth down one and setteth up another," our text declares. That is the rule of life. Man cannot disregard God with impunity. False ambition carries within it the seeds of its own destruction. But true ambition is blessed by God, who judges the heart. And all true ambition finds its source and its object in the Cross.

PSALM 77:6: *"I call to remembrance my song in the night; I commune with mine own heart, and my spirit made diligent search."*

SONGS IN THE NIGHT

The night is a time of mystery, of dread, of evil deeds. Men have always feared the night and have taken elaborate precautions against the dangers that lurk in the darkness. In our day we have coined a flippant phrase to describe the artificial courage that men summon to ward off these fears of the unknown. "Whistling in the dark," we call it.

The Christian, however, does not have to "whistle in the dark." He dispels his fears with a better melody. He sings "songs in the night." Hymns of praise, thankfulness, and trust well from the Christian heart. This is the best antidote for fear.

The night is also a time for introspection. After the bustle and din of the day we can pause to take stock of our deeds and misdeeds and to think long thoughts of the morrow. Like the psalmist, in the night we can "commune with our own heart" and let our spirit "make diligent search."

Such self-examination is a wholesome spiritual

61

exercise. Busy as we are, we are really never too busy for meditation, for prayer, for giving thought to God. When night's shadows fall, it is good to remember Him — His guidance during the day, His ceaseless care, and His multiplied blessings. His love for us makes us sing — to break into "songs in the night."

The night is a time, too, for relaxation. Men like to relax by singing, to shed the cares of the day with song. Songs of joy, songs of fellowship have their place.

But there are some songs that men sing in the night that indeed belong to the realm of spiritual night. Their music inflames man's baser nature. Their words offend the Christian's high and pure ideals.

Such songs do not cross the Christian's lips or resound in the Christian's home. He, too, sings "songs in the night," but his songs do honor to God and express the joy of the Christian life.

Songs filled the night when Christ was born. The angels' music made the heavens ring. Those celestial hymns should strike a chord in each Christian heart. They should find their echo in the songs that we sing in the night.

PSALM 87:7: *"All my springs are in Thee."*

THE SPRINGS OF LIFE

A spring of clear, fresh, sparkling water is a joyful sight to behold. It gives refreshment to the parched wayfarer. It sends its stream down the mountainside. It waters the earth and makes it green. It is a symbol of life.

The spring has its source deep in the earth. No man produced it; no human device brings the water forth. It is a process of nature, men say. But the Christian knows that when men say "nature," they really mean "God."

And so the Christian, like the psalmist, can say of himself as he extols the mercy of God: "All my springs are in Thee!" Our life has its source deep in the love and wisdom of God. In the Christian life the divine love and wisdom spring forth in a clear, fresh, life-giving stream.

The Christian's daily life will be sanctified by this thought: "All my springs are in Thee!" And he will apply this truth to every experience, every relationship.

"In Thee is the spring of *knowledge*" — the saving knowledge which comes alone through the enlightenment of the Holy Spirit; the knowledge of Christ as the crucified and risen Savior; the knowledge that makes men wise unto salvation; the knowledge that is not an attainment of the intellect but a union of the heart with God.

"In Thee is the spring of *courage*" — courage to face the evil day; courage to bear the wearisome burdens of life; courage to meet without dismay the trials and disappointments that beset our path; courage to confront both grief and pain; courage to say, "In all these things we are more than conquerors through Him who loved us!"

"In Thee is the spring of *hope*" — hope in a dark and anxious hour; hope that bids our fears subside, our worry cease; hope that clings to the assurance that the blank walls of men are the open doors of God; hope that "maketh not ashamed" — because its springs are in Him.

"In Thee is the spring of *love*" — love in a world of tears and hate; love that extends even to our enemies; love that flows from Him who, while we were yet sinners, sent His Son to die for us; love that shone forth from a rude cross and an open tomb.

"In Thee is the spring of *life*" — the life that is hid with Christ in God; the life that is truly abundant; the life that knows no ending; the life that comes from knowing Thee, the only true God, and Jesus Christ, whom Thou hast sent.

> Thou of life the Fountain art,
> Freely let me take of Thee;
> Spring Thou up within my heart,
> Rise to all eternity.

LAMENT OF THE LONELY

Life holds many depressing experiences. There are many times when we are brought low. Life seems especially bleak when we are lonely.

Man is a social creature. It is natural for him to seek companionship. He wants and needs friends. He longs to be understood, to be appreciated, to be loved. "Nobody loves me!" is a pathetic cry. Children utter it when they are piqued. But have we not all felt gloomy when the world seemed hostile, friends forsook us, and trusted comrades failed?

Even the psalmist felt such loneliness. His cry is heart-rending: "There was no man that would know me . . . no man cared for my soul." He was not just feeling sorry for himself. He was pierced to his inmost depths by the awful realization: "I am all alone!"

And so the psalmist lamented over his loneliness. No friends were there to stand by him, none to share his burden, none to listen to his woes, none to plead his cause. Well could he groan: "Refuge failed me!"

We can bear a good many ills more readily than loneliness. The cure for loneliness is not just having people around us. We can be lonely in a teeming city or in a gay, chattering crowd. The cure for loneliness is to have people who think of us — with concern, with interest, with love. The greatest pathos lies in the psalmist's words — and we can almost hear him sob — "No man cared for my soul!"

We shall usually not be lonely, however, unless we allow ourselves to be lonely. If we want others to be interested in us, we must be interested in others. If we want to be loved, we must love. If we want men to care for our soul, we must care for men's souls. That kind of life is never lonely.

"Refuge failed me; no man cared for my soul!" the psalmist complained. But that was not quite true. In the next verse after our text he takes hold of himself, turns to God, and confesses: "Thou art my Refuge and my Portion in the land of the living!"

He is our Refuge, too. With Him at our side, we are never alone — neither in life nor in death. We shall never be lonely, because, for our sakes, He was lonely on the cross.

PSALM 56:8: *"Thou tellest my wanderings; put Thou my tears into Thy
bottle. Are they not in Thy book?"*

A BOTTLE OF TEARS

In this strange but comforting passage
the psalmist talks about four things: wanderings, tears,
a bottle, and a book. The wanderings and the tears are
ours. The bottle and the book are God's. That is a poetic
way of telling the story of our life and our relationship
to God.

Wanderings indicate confusion, uncertainty, error.
If we always followed the straight, unbending line of
God's commandments, we would never wander. Our
goal would always be clear, our steps would always be
firm, and our course would always be straight. But sin
blinds our eyes to the goal and turns our footsteps into
the byways. And so we lose our way and wander aimlessly — confused at first, desperate at last.

But there is One who sees that we are lost, and
He sends His own Son to rescue us. With such a Guide
we find our way again and travel on.

Tears means sorrow. We all shed many tears during
our lifetime. We weep over our griefs, our pains, our

disappointments, our sins. It is human to cry. Even Jesus wept. For the Christian, tears should be a sign of repentance, which leads to "salvation not to be repented of."

A *bottle* is for preservation. God, says the psalmist, keeps our tears in a bottle. What a strange picture!

Strange, but consoling. Among certain Oriental peoples the tears of the mourners were kept in a bottle as a memorial to the departed one. And thus God keeps in memory the tears we have shed over our sins and our infirmities. It hurts when we slay the "old man" within us; it makes us weep in remorse. But God remembers our weeping. That is the kind of sacrifice that He desires. Every tear we shed awakens His compassion.

A *book* is for remembrance. In God's book are written all our deeds, both evil and good. But all our sins are crossed out in God's book with a mighty X — the cross of Jesus Christ. And so the only thing that remains in that volume is the story of His love — that love which finds expression in the good that we do, in the service that we render Him. In His book our names have been stenciled with the blood of Jesus Christ.

PSALM 120:6, 7: *"My soul hath long dwelt with him that hateth peace. I am for peace; but when I speak, they are for war."*

DEBATING WITH WARMONGERS

It would be pleasant, we often think, to be able to get away from the humdrum, irksome tasks and associations of our everyday life. It would be a relief if we never had to do unpleasant things, to listen to unpleasant words, to deal with unpleasant people. And there are so many that fall into this category!

But life is not that way. Our station in life is just that place in which God has put us for the purpose of exercising our Christian love and of demonstrating our Christian faith. Even our Lord, in His high-priestly prayer, asked His heavenly Father not to take His disciples out of the world, but to keep them from the evil in the world.

And there is so much evil in the world! We echo the psalmist's complaint: "My soul hath long dwelt with him that hateth peace." Unless we are singularly fortunate, it is the lot of most Christians to work in the company of those who are worldly, unbelieving, antagonistic to Christian faith and Christian ideals. Whether we like it or not, we have to adjust ourselves to dwelling — or associating — "with him that hateth peace," the peace that is found in the Christian Gospel.

We feel the opposition of the world especially when we speak up in behalf of our faith. With the psalmist we can say: "I am for peace." Yet we also share his experience that "when I speak, they are for war."

Discouraging, isn't it? To bear witness to the glad tidings of peace in Christ, only to meet with a rebuff, mockery, hostility. The children of this world simply do not want to accept the peace of Christ. They prefer the ways of the world, "the fleshly lusts that war against the soul." They may not always realize it, but they are at war with God. That indeed is their natural state.

The devil is the original warmonger. From his malign influence flow all the evil, all the strife, all the hatred that set man against his fellow man; all the petty quarrels and jealousies that are magnified at last into the cosmic tragedy of war. War in the temporal realm is just the outward manifestation and result of war in the spiritual realm.

In the midst of men who "are for war," Christians must be men of peace. We must reflect in our peaceable dealings with our fellow men the inner peace that prevails in our soul. If there is anything that can turn away wrath, it is the soft answer — the answer that is drawn from the Gospel of peace.

To say, "I am for peace," does not mean that we desire peace only for ourselves. It implies that we seek to impart the spirit of peace to others — especially to those who "are for war." To say, "I am for peace," means as much as to say, "I am for God."

That is why Jesus calls the peacemakers blessed. It is they who shall be called the children of God.

PSALM 139:23, 24: *"Search me, O God, and know my heart; try me, and know my thoughts; and see if there be any wicked way in me, and lead me in the way everlasting."*

THE DIVINELY EXAMINED LIFE

Persons who have something to hide, whose past life will not bear close and critical scrutiny, have been taking refuge behind the Fifth Amendment. They will not submit to searching questions which will tend, if answered honestly, to incriminate them. Their very reluctance to answer creates strong suspicion of their guilt.

There is no place in God's kingdom for "Fifth Amendment Christians." The Christian is willing to expose himself fully to the searching light of God's Law. With Hagar he declares: "Thou, God, seest me." He echoes the words of David in the magnificent psalm from which our text is taken: "O Lord, Thou hast searched me and known me. Thou knowest my downsitting and mine uprising, Thou understandest my thought afar off."

The Christian has nothing to hide from God because he knows that ultimately there is nothing he *can* hide from God. He can put up a false front with his fellow men. He can veil his real intentions and disguise his motives in his relationships with other people. But not so with God. He realizes that God knows his heart, perceives his thoughts. And so the Christian willingly submits to the divine scrutiny.

He does so in the full consciousness that what God sees within him will not be wholly pleasant or noble or pure. In fact, what God sees in the heart in its natural state is wholly corrupt and alien to God. What God sees in the human heart will not dispose Him to forgive and save the sinner.

And yet God *does* forgive and save the sinner. Such redemption is surely an act of unmerited grace. The Christian must confess, in the words of the well-known hymn: "I know that, though in doing good I spend my life, I never could Atone for all I've done." God looks on us with favor only because He looks with the eyes of love. By the power of that love we are transformed.

That transformation includes repentance. The Christian says with the psalmist: "See if there be any wicked way in me." That is a contrite prayer, and an honest one as well. There is no self-righteousness there; we confess that we are wicked. There is no pride there, or self-delusion. We have seen ourselves in the mirror of God's Law, and the sight is not pretty.

And so, repentant and believing, we turn to Him in whom alone there is help. To Him we pray, "Lead me in the way everlasting." We ask Him to lead us in a way that we cannot find of ourselves. We ask Him to lead us along the way that begins at His cross and that ends at His throne.

PSALM 10:4, 11: *"The wicked, through the pride of his countenance, will not seek after God; God is not in all his thoughts. . . . He hath said in his heart, God hath forgotten; He hideth his face; He will never see it."*

THE MARK OF THE PRACTICAL ATHEIST

We hear much nowadays about the besmirching of reputations. The epithet "fellow traveler" arouses resentment on the part of the person who is the object of that term. The fact that his frequent association with communists and his professed sympathy with their objectives may have brought this stigma upon him does not seem to impress him.

Most people would likewise regard their reputation to have been marred if they were called "atheists." The fact that they do not openly disavow God or deny His existence seems to safeguard them against any such accusation. Their manner of life, however — their complete indifference to God, their open flouting of His commands — brands them as "fellow travelers" with the cause of atheism. They may not be professional atheists, but to all intents and purposes they are practical atheists.

The mark of the practical atheist is *pride*. "The wicked, through the pride of his countenance, will not

73

seek after God," says the psalmist. Pride is the fundamental sin. Pride is self-love, self-will. From the sin of pride all the other sins derive their source.

Man in his pride does not seek after God. He seeks after himself. His own pleasure, his own gain, his own honor — these are the objects of his quest. Truly, "God is not in all his thoughts." His thoughts are fully occupied with himself. The result is the same as though he would openly say, "There is no God."

The practical atheist says in his heart, "God hath forgotten; He hideth His face; he will never see it." Man in his pride thinks that he can "pull the wool over the eyes of God." For practical purposes, he acts as though God did not exist. At best he regards God as some blind, abstract, impersonal force. And so he gives free rein to his own aims and desires. Pride seeks always to "get by" with whatever it pleases.

But the way of pride is the way of folly. The wise man is he who echoes Hagar's words: "Thou, God, seest me," and who lives in the awareness of continuing scrutiny of the all-seeing, all-knowing God.

That God has chosen, however, not to look upon our naked sin, but to veil it with His saving grace. That grace is ours through the shed blood of Christ. That grace is ours through faith in His Son.

PSALM 19:12: *"Who can understand his errors? Cleanse Thou me from secret faults."*

WE MUST BARE OUR SOULS

Psychology is an absorbing study. The word itself really means "the study of the soul." By means of this science, men have sought to analyze the workings of the human mind, the motivations for human behavior, the inner springs of human conduct.

Psychology, however, does not hold the complete and final answer to all problems of the inner life. Psychology must be guided and sanctified by a higher, surer science: *theology.* Thus the psalmist could not turn to the psychologist for an answer to his tormenting question: "Who can understand his errors?" That answer can be supplied alone by the sure, unerring Word of God.

And the answer that the divine Word gives is simply: "No one." Sin has so pervaded our life, so corrupted our emotions, so distorted our sense of values, that no man can truly and fully comprehend the extent of his sinfulness or the exact nature of each error that he commits. This fact becomes all the more appalling as

75

we realize that so many of our faults are sins of omission, of sheer neglect, of our inability to understand the scope and the demands of the divine obligations which rest upon each of us.

Thus we must cry with the psalmist: "Who can understand his errors?" The question really supplies its own answer. We must, in all honesty, respond: "Not I, O Lord!"

Our only recourse, then, is to place our trust in the psalmist's Lord and ours — a Lord who is ever more ready to forgive than we are to pray, a Lord who knows us better than we know ourselves, a Lord who bore all our sins, known and unknown, upon the cross.

And to that Lord we can also pray: "Cleanse Thou me from secret faults." If we could expect forgiveness only for those sins that we can recall, or if the Lord demanded of us a complete accounting of each specific sin, then indeed despair would be our lot.

But the Savior who died on Calvary atoned as well for our secret faults — the sins that are known to Him alone and to us, and perhaps not even to us.

It is easy for us to abstain from gross and violent sins. It is most likely that murder, adultery, and robbery shall never be laid to our charge. But the *secret* sins — ah, they are just as real and just as damning in the eyes of a holy God. For these sins, too, we need the cleansing blood.

In that blood we shall be made clean. Through His love we shall be made pure. Before His throne we shall stand arrayed in white.

Psalm 11:3: *"If the foundations be destroyed, what can the righteous do?"*

THE NEED OF SOCIAL STABILITY

Foundations are important. If you have seen a house, a church, or a public building under construction, you will have observed the great amount of time and care devoted to the laying of the foundation of that structure. Solid foundations mean solid buildings.

The rule that holds good in constructing a building holds equally good in constructing a life, both the life of an individual and the life of society.

At times we see people floundering about, groping for direction. "They have no roots," we say. They have laid no solid foundation for their life. They have trusted in their own resources, or they have been afraid to face reality, or they have lived only for the day. Their life is built on shifting sands.

The righteous man builds differently. He does not construct his life on the uncertain foundation of his own mind, talents, or strength. Such foundations will sooner or later be destroyed. He rather builds on the unshakable promises of God, guaranteed by the redeeming sacrifice and the measureless love of His Son.

The same principle holds true with regard to men when they live and act in a group — the "social order," as we call it. The alarm is being sounded today that society is disintegrating. Wars and rumors of war, social injustices, class and racial antagonisms, the lowering of the standards of morality and virtue, the rising divorce rate, juvenile delinquency — all these are signs that the foundations of our social order are crumbling.

Why are they crumbling? Because men have forgotten God and have gloried in the forgetting. Because men have put their trust in scientific progress, in educational theories, in international pacts, in the idea of basic goodness.

When these foundations are destroyed, what shall the righteous do? He will build his life, his home, his vocation, upon the solid rock of God's Word. He will influence his homeland to follow truth, justice, morality, and God's peace.

In this course alone lies peace for our soul, security for our land, and peace for our troubled world.

PSALM 68:6: *"God setteth the solitary in families; He bringeth out those which are bound with chains; but the rebellious dwell in a dry land."*

SOLACE FOR THE SOLITARY

One of the major tragedies of war is the displaced person — and his number is legion — who has lost home, family, job, and who is thrown upon the mercies of an unfriendly, unfeeling world. His life has been torn up by the very roots; he has no feeling of security; he has lost almost his very identity.

By nature we are all displaced persons, displaced from the kingdom of God. We have been driven out, not by any quirk of unkind fate, but by the dread power of sin within us. Deprived of God's presence, bereft of our heritage, we feel rootless, restless, solitary.

But we are not doomed to remain in exile. The psalmist speaks an assuring word of purest Gospel: "God setteth the solitary in families." By the redeeming grace in Christ, the Lord reclaims us from the alien realm of darkness; He frees us from the captivity of sin. "He bringeth out those which are bound with chains," the psalmist exults.

This is God's own repatriation program. Redeemed

by His Son, we are solitary no longer. We are set into the family of God; we join the fellowship of His saints; we are members of the household of faith. Here is security, peace, and freedom indeed — here in the goodly company of the redeemed.

There is another side of this picture, however. "The rebellious dwell in a dry land," says the psalmist. There are some who refuse to be repatriated into the realm of light. They prefer to remain exiled from God. They choose the dry wastes of sin rather than the green pastures of grace. And so they are doomed to the eternal solitude of the lost.

But those who dwell with God are never alone. Though unknown, unwanted, forsaken by men, the Christian is known to God, wanted by God, set by God into the midst of His own elect family. In the circle of that family we shall forever be at home.

PSALM 130:4: *"But there is forgiveness with Thee, that Thou mayest be feared."*

GRACE ANTICIPATES PIETY

A recent book on theology bears the title "Let God Be God." It is not, of course, within the power or province of man to establish the existence or nature of God. It is a mark of God that He is completely self-sufficient.

Rather, the point is that man must recognize God to be what He is. What is more, man must recognize God's exclusive right to be what He is. Man must not usurp God's place. It is a human tendency to spell "God" with a small "g" and "man" with a capital "M." That is sheer idolatry.

To "let God be God" means to recognize His *grace.* That grace shows itself in forgiveness. "There is forgiveness with Thee," the psalmist confesses. Grace means undeserved love. It extends itself to one who is completely unworthy. It expects nothing in return.

A mother's love will forgive a wayward child. A loving father will welcome home the returning prodigal. That is noble indeed. But God's love is still nobler. Human love and human forgiveness, be it ever so complete, so genuine, so warm, still bears the taint of self-interest. Nothing human is perfect.

God is different. Nothing is lacking in His grace, His forgiveness. "Plenteous grace with Thee is found, Grace to cover all my sin," we sing. Because God is God, we are forgiven.

This is not just a comfortable thought. It must be an inner dynamic. To be forgiven does not mean simply to enjoy a warm feeling within. It means that we become completely different. Forgiven, we make a spiritual U turn.

The psalmist describes this total inner change as the fear of God. Hence to "let God be God" also means to live in His *fear*. "That Thou mayest be feared," he writes. God's forgiving grace produces piety. The forgiven man is God's man. God's man, fearing Him, is pious.

The motive of Christian piety is not the hope of reward or the escape from punishment. It is the love of Christ. With His love in our hearts, we live in His forgiveness, and we serve in His fear.

The fear of God, of course, does not mean something slavish. It means something childlike. We show that we fear God by loving Him, serving Him, living His kind of life.

The Christian does not honor God by seeing how little he can "get by with." God will not settle for the minimum. Nothing less than the maximum will do Him honor. "Love so amazing, so divine, Demands my soul, my life, my all."

PSALM 91:7: *"A thousand shall fall at thy side, and ten thousand at thy right hand; but it shall not come nigh thee."*

FAITH SCALES THE UNSCALABLE

As these lines are written, a long holiday weekend is beginning. The radio is sounding forth the insistent warning: "Be careful!" "Drive safely!" "Be alive next Tuesday!" Despite these urgent pleas, it is safe to make the tragic prediction that several hundred persons will meet accidental death during these days.

Will none of these victims be Christians? Must we assume that all those who meet violent death, like those in the Gospel upon whom the tower of Siloam fell, are especially sinful and without God in their lives? "Of course not!" we indignantly protest. In the experiences of us all, we have known dear children of God who have lost their lives in tragic accidents.

What, then, does the psalmist mean when he gives the sweeping assurance: "A thousand shall fall at thy side, and ten thousand at thy right hand; but it shall not come nigh thee"? It all depends, of course, upon the meaning of the little word "it." *"It* shall not come nigh thee." What is *it?*

It, of course, means *evil.* Come plague or pestilence, war or destruction, no evil shall befall God's children. That is the whole burden of the magnificent 91st Psalm, from which this text is taken. The psalmist makes it crystal clear in the words that follow our text: "There shall no evil befall thee." That is God's promise — sure, clear, abiding. His ways with us are always good. His judgment is better than ours.

Well, then, is the Christian sick? Sickness is God's blessing in disguise. Does the Christian suffer loss? In Christ we have imperishable gain. Does the Christian meet an accident? For the Christian there are no accidents, for He who marks the sparrow's fall guides every step of our way. Does the Christian die? Death in Christ is blest repose and the portal to endless joy.

Gladly, then, we can take to ourselves the divine promise: "A thousand shall fall at thy side, and ten thousand at thy right hand, but it shall not come nigh thee" — no evil, no darkness, no fear. Dwelling in His secret place, we indeed "abide under the shadow of the Almighty" — on the highway and in our homes, on the job and hard at play, in time of war and in time of peace, when skies are clear and when clouds hang low, in life and in the hour of death. "In Him will I trust!" we exult with the psalmist — even when a thousand fall at our side and ten thousand at our right hand.

PSALM 131:1: *"Lord, my heart is not haughty nor mine eyes lofty; neither do I exercise myself in great matters or in things too high for me."*

LORD, CURB MY AMBITIONS!

Pride is the basic human sin. Pride is really the love of self, the placing of our own needs and ambitions and cravings into the forefront. God and our neighbor are crowded out. From the sin of thinking first of ourselves flows every other sin and the breaking of every commandment. This is the great idolatry.

Pride is the opposite of love. Love thinks first of the other person — his welfare, his interests. Love comes from God; love is the very nature of God. And as love is the fulfillment of God's Law, pride is the breaking of God's Law — all of it. For through pride we actually set ourselves up in place of God and ahead of Him. And God says: "Thou shalt have no other gods before Me!"

The psalmist's confession should be our own: "Lord, my heart is not haughty nor mine eyes lofty." Can we honestly say that? Is our heart properly disposed? Are our eyes properly focused? The heart filled with the

85

Savior's love will not be haughty. The eyes fixed upon Calvary's cross will not be lofty.

Love alone is the antidote to pride, the cure for selfish ambition. Love thinks of the neighbor first; love is faithful to its work; love sets a good example; love holds no grudges; love is true and modest and pure. Love has no other gods before the true God.

Sinful pride exalts and worships an idol: the capital letter *I*. But when the Spirit of God moves into our heart, He cancels that *I* and makes of it a cross.

Thus transformed, we can echo the psalmist's words: "Neither do I exercise myself in great matters or in things too high for me." The Christian knows that there are things too great, too high for him. These are the things of God, whose judgments are unsearchable and His ways past finding out. Our reason and our physical prowess are limited; there are bounds beyond which puny, finite man cannot trespass. Man, realizing this fact, has little cause for pride. Humbly and reverently, he will not exercise himself in great matters or in things too high for him.

God wants to put man in his place. That place is at the foot of the cross.

PSALM 95:6: *"Oh, come, let us worship and bow down; let us kneel before the Lord, our Maker."*

OUR KNEES MUST LEARN
TO BEND

Kneeling is the posture of humility. Those knees of ours — how rigid they are, how stiff with pride! How hard it is to bow to authority; how hard to bow to the better counsel and wisdom of our elders; how hard to bow in apology to those whom we have wronged!

But just because it is hard, it is a wholesome Christian exercise, a practice that will strengthen our spiritual muscles, that will tone up our spiritual life. Our knees will be flexible if we bend them enough, and as a result we'll be able to walk along life's pathway with more spring and firmness in our step.

And most of all, we must bow the knee to God. Not a routine and hurried genuflection, as is the custom in some churches, but a genuine posture of repentance and humility before the Lord, our Maker, whom we have sorely grieved by our sins of thought, word, and deed. In the recalling of these sins we scarce can lift to Him our weeping eyes, and so we fall on our knees and beg His mercy.

When we kneel, we give up our pride; we bow in the dust of remorse and self-abasement; we acknowledge the presence and the authority of One who is greater and better than we — for a man kneels only to one who is superior to him. And in that act of humility we find true honor; in that self-abasement we are exalted; and in that posture of weakness we find strength, strength from our loving and forgiving God.

Kneeling is also the posture of prayer. To be sure, we can pray in any position; but kneeling is perhaps the most conducive to real, undisturbed meditation. And kneeling, too, is the posture that best symbolizes our relationship to God.

And so we kneel, not in a perfunctory, empty gesture, but in true devotion, as we pour out our souls in prayer. Prayer for the needs and problems of the day; prayer for strength against temptation; prayer for our friends and loved ones; prayer for those who are weak and need our help.

Thus, the more we kneel, the stronger we grow in our own Christian life and in our spiritual fellowship. Ever stronger in Him at whose name "every knee shall bow . . . and every tongue shall confess that Jesus Christ is Lord."

PSALM 147:3, 4: *"He healeth the broken in heart and bindeth up their wounds. He telleth the number of the stars; He calleth them all by their names."*

THE STARS AND THE SCARS

God did not merely create the universe en masse. He gave particular care to each individual item of His creative work. He marks each falling sparrow, He nourishes each tender plant. Indeed, says the psalmist: "He telleth the number of the stars; He calleth them all by their names."

That God who has called into being all the hosts of heaven and keeps them in their appointed course is not too high and not too busy to know and to care for you and me. And not just to know who we are and that we are. He knows every thought, He feels every pain, He watches every step, He hears every sigh — of all of us, at all times.

And so the psalmist says: "He healeth the broken in heart and bindeth up their wounds." Is your heart broken? I don't mean from some trivial matter, as we loosely use the expression, "My heart is broken." But is your heart broken by sin? Do you really grieve over the offense that you have given your God? Are

89

you truly sitting in the sackcloth and ashes of true repentance?

The message of the Cross is that God heals our broken heart. He sent His Son to live and suffer and die upon the cross, that through His stripes we may be healed.

And even as He heals the heart that is broken by sin, so He binds up the wounds in its wake: all our griefs, our pains, our shattered hopes, our broken friendships, our failures, are the result of sin — sin in the world, sin in our own heart.

But He sees our wounds, sore and bleeding. And so He stoops down and binds them up with the healing emollient of His love. He is the great Physician, "who makes the wounded spirit whole and calms the troubled breast."

There we have it: the Lord of the rolling spheres is the Lord of the broken heart. He who knows the names of the stars knows your name and mine. He speaks our name and bids our fears subside, our sorrows cease. He speaks our name and gently draws us to Himself. He knows our needs; He remembers that we are dust. He is ever more ready to hear than we are to pray. All through life He will guide us with His counsel and afterward receive us into glory.

That is the kind of Lord that we have — the psalmist's Lord and ours. A Lord who fashioned the panoply of heaven; a Lord who hung upon a tree. For He who holds the stars in His hands is He who bears the scars in His hands.

PSALM 18:28, 29: *"For Thou wilt light my candle; the Lord, my God, will enlighten my darkness. For by Thee I have run through a troop; and by my God have I leaped over a wall."*

A LIGHT AND A LEAP

We all know what it feels like to go into a dark room. We feel our way, we grope around, we bruise our shins. Darkness is nothing pleasant. A child cries in the dark. A thief prowls in the dark. We lose our way in the dark.

When we are in darkness, there is just one thing that we want: light. Any kind of light — an electric bulb, a flashlight, a match, a candle. When the light glows, we feel safe and sure of ourselves again.

We have all felt the fear of physical darkness. But the terror is far greater when the spirit is dark. Sin brings darkness to our soul. Every time we sin we snuff out the light of God's grace. Every time we sin we plunge ourselves into darkness, so that we stumble, grope, fall.

In our darkness we can't find the light ourselves. So we turn to God and say to Him with the psalmist: "Thou wilt light my candle; the Lord, my God, will enlighten my darkness."

91

His grace makes our candle burn. By that light the shades of night are chased away. The candle may flicker at times. Our faith may waver. Doubts may assail us. Sin may blind our eyes to the heavenly rays.

But God keeps the candle burning. Its flame dispels our darkness. Its glow illumines our heavenward way. Its light shines from the Cross.

But now the psalmist abruptly changes the picture and turns to a different comparison. He knows that we aren't only beset by sin, but that we are also oppressed by difficulties and obstacles as we make our way through life.

And so he cries: "By Thee I have run through a troop; and by my God have I leaped over a wall." David sees his enemies lined up before him in a troop; with God's help he will run through them. He sees his way blocked by a wall; with God's help he will leap over it.

Is your way blocked by a troop? Do problems and difficulties in your life loom up before you and make you quake? Do you feel like throwing up your hands in surrender?

These are walls, to be sure. But walls can be hurdled. Not by our own mind or muscles, indeed; but with the power that God infuses into us. With His help we can make the hurdle. And then we shall look back and say: "By my God have I leaped over a wall."

He gives us light; He gives us strength. David knew it; we shall learn it, too.

PSALM 24:10: *"Who is this King of Glory? The Lord of Hosts, He is the King of Glory."*

WHO IS THIS KING OF GLORY?

There is a proverb of the African natives that says: "A well-worn path must lead to a great king." For almost two thousand years the children of men have been following the path to Bethlehem. It's a well-worn path by this time, and it leads to a King who is great indeed, greater than any mortal who has ever worn the royal purple. He is the King of Glory, at whose feet all the tribes of men must lay their trophies, as they crown Him Lord of all.

Not all men, sad to say, join in that homage. An old Greek myth tells of Prometheus, who defied and scorned the gods by stealing the heavenly fire from Mount Olympus. For punishment he was bound to a rock, where to all eternity the birds of the air come to pluck away at his vitals.

In the same spirit of pride, many men today flout the true and living God. They try to steal the fire from off His altar. They covet, then claim for themselves what belongs to God — wisdom, power, glory.

93

They are chained to the rock they have hewn for themselves.

The King of Glory shows us a better way: "Not by power, nor by might, but by My Spirit, saith the Lord of Hosts." In His Spirit alone do we find the key to happy, abundant living. His Spirit is love and truth and forgiveness. His Spirit alone opens to us the gates of glory.

By the King's command the glorious gates swing wide anew. And through those welcoming portals stream all the weary, sin-ridden sons of men who have seen the star of the King and have hastened to kneel at His throne. Hither come the fugitive from the storm and strife, the pilgrim along life's tortuous road, to find in Him the haven of rest.

This is the King of Glory: our Savior, God's own Son. Once He came in meekness; daily He comes in grace; at the end He will come in glory.

May this be our constant prayer: O King of Glory, establish in our hearts Thy throne, and rule us by Thy love!

TIMES AND SEASONS

> PSALM 84:7: *"They go from strength to strength; every one of them in Zion appeareth before God."*

FROM STRENGTH TO STRENGTH

We have just crossed the threshold of the new year. We have never traveled this way before. The road is uncertain and dark. The pathway is winding and steep. The outcome is veiled and obscure.

Such a prospect might fill us with dread. Well it might, if we should travel this way alone. But the Christian has a constant Guide, who knows every step of the way. With Him at our side, we shall not stumble or fall. Our step is sure and our heart serene as we travel the uncharted way.

For this we have the assurance of divine promise and the example of God's people through the ages. The psalmist put it thus: "They go from strength to strength." Alone we are impotent, helpless, confused. Alone we sink, we faint, we fall. But God is our Refuge and Strength. He bears our burden, solves our problem, charts our course.

And He imparts His strength to us always at just the right time and in just the right measure. This is the

97

best antidote for worry. He has never failed us in the past. He will never fail us in the future — not if we put our trust in Him. He says to us each passing day: "My grace is sufficient for thee, for My strength is made perfect in weakness."

Our best-laid plans will come to naught unless we have His blessing. Our worried concern for tomorrow's needs will bring us no guarantee of food or raiment, health or wealth. All our bounties come from Him. He has given us His strength in the past. And from the remembrance of that past strength we go on to the assurance of new strength for the future.

The psalmist, however, goes on to indicate the source of this strength. Speaking of God's people, he declares: "Every one of them in Zion appeareth before God." We draw our strength from God. And thus we must seek Him where He is to be found: in Zion, in His church, in the means of grace — the holy Word and Sacraments.

There we must appear before Him. We come before Him as humble penitents, seeking His pardon, receiving His grace. We come before Him as earnest suppliants, pleading our need, receiving His bounty. We come before Him as redeemed children, hymning His praises, receiving His love.

In Zion we find Him; in Zion we serve Him; in Zion we live with Him — in the strength that is ours as the sons of God.

PSALM 147:16, 17: *"He giveth snow like wool; He scattereth the hoarfrost like ashes. He casteth forth His ice like morsels; who can stand before His cold?"*

THE LORD OF WINTER'S ICE AND SNOW

Most of the land, these winter days, is covered with a blanket of white. New Year's Day always conjures up pictures of snowy fields, icy winds, and a fire blazing in the hearth. It makes life a bit more rugged, but it makes the earth more beautiful, too. That is God's own compensation.

And so, looking out upon the winter landscape, we are reminded of the question that God once addressed to Job: "Hast thou entered into the treasures of the snow?" Treasures are there, indeed, and we shall find them if we seek.

In the snow we find the treasure of God's *providence.* He who designed the snowflake, delicate and complex as it is, designs your life and mine in a pattern just as sure and just as wise.

We see that providence at work in nature. God

99

sends the snow and the ice to cover the earth, to give warmth and moisture to the seed below. When spring-time comes, that seed will spring up and yield its fruit.

Our lives are that way, too. When we are buffeted by the gales of adversity and chilled by fears and doubts, the winter often seems long indeed, and springtime far behind. But in God's good time the sun of His mercy shines again, and the seeds of hope spring forth. We cannot know the warmth of spring unless we have first felt winter's chill.

That is God's way of dealing with us. Grace follows sin; hope follows despair; joy follows grief; life follows death. It is true in nature. It is just as true in the Christian life.

In the snow we find also the treasure of God's *purity*. "Pure as the driven snow" is more than a figure of speech. It is God's own way of picturing the spiritual purity that is ours through Christ. "Though your sins be as scarlet," His prophet assures us, "they shall be as white as snow."

Think of that promise the next time you look out upon the snow. It makes the earth look pure and clean. It cloaks the grime and the ugliness below. White is the color of beauty.

And white is the color of God. He covers the filthy rags of our sin with the white and shining garb of the merits of His Son, which we put on by faith. And so, by grace, "we are pure as He is pure."

The robe that we wear is made white — because the robe that He wore was made red.

> PSALM 51:16, 17: *"For Thou desirest not sacrifice, else would I give it; Thou delightest not in burnt offering. The sacrifices of God are a broken spirit; a broken and a contrite heart, O God, Thou wilt not despise."*

THE BETTER SACRIFICE

We are standing at the threshold of Lent. To a large segment of Christendom, Lent means sacrifice — the obligation to give up certain kinds of food, certain kinds of pleasure during this forty-day period. This, it is asserted, is "self-denial."

In the Old Testament period people also had the idea that they could please God by means of mere outward acts of self-mortification: fasting, special offerings, special prayers. But the psalmist is explicit in showing how this type of religious performance will never satisfy God. "Thou desirest not sacrifice," he writes, "else would I give it; Thou delightest not in burnt offering."

True religion does not consist in mere externals, in the mere rote performance of churchly duties, in abstaining from certain types of food or recreation for a few weeks out of the year. This is not what self-denial truly means. It means denying one's *self*.

What God expects of us, therefore — not merely

101

during Lent but throughout the year and throughout our life — is not merely the outward amenities that men associate with "being religious." He is not honored by a superficial and temporary show of piety. What He wants of us — now and always — is *ourselves*.

This the psalmist further explains when he emphasizes: "The sacrifices of God are a broken spirit; a broken and a contrite heart, O God, Thou wilt not despise." We must take the spirit of our fleshly pride and let it be broken beneath the hammer blows of God's Law. We must take our heart — from which all evil thoughts proceed — and let it be purified by the cleansing power of the Savior's blood. We must take our life and let it be sanctified by the indwelling presence of God's Spirit. Anew we must learn that we belong to Him.

Contrition, repentance, faith, love, service — with such sacrifices God is well pleased. Such an offering He will not despise.

We can offer Him nothing more. He expects of us nothing less.

Lent II

> PSALM 75:8: *"For in the hand of the Lord there is a cup, and the wine is red; it is full of mixture, and He poureth out of the same; but the dregs thereof, all the wicked of the earth shall wring them out and drink them."*

THE CUP IN THE LORD'S HAND

The Scriptures, in their poetic style, often speak of human life and experience as a "cup." "My cup runneth over," exclaims the psalmist as he reflects upon the abundant mercies of God. "Are ye able to drink of the cup that I shall drink of?" asks our Lord of His disciples, as He warns them of the trials to come.

The Lord's hand holds a cup, as it were, and each of us must drink of it. The wine therein is red and full of mixture. The Christian life is not unalloyed bliss and freedom from care. The Christian is not destined to sip only sweet ambrosia day after day. He must drink the strong red wine in the Lord's cup. The pleasures of that cup are mixed with pain and tears.

God's Son Himself had a cup to drink. The Lenten Season reminds us of the bitterness of His cup. Momentarily He shrank from it; but, strengthened from on high, He could bravely say: "The cup which My Father hath given Me, shall I not drink it?"

Because He drank that cup for us, we can drink it, too. His strength makes firm the hands that quiver as they hold the cup. His peace makes still the heart that quails at the very thought of it. His love makes sweet the bitter taste of it. His grace makes only the blessings of it to remain.

When the cup has been emptied, the dregs remain. They remain for the wicked to consume, says the psalmist. The cup of life may seem pleasant to the worldling. He drinks the heady nectar with a flourish. He thinks the warm glow will last.

But it does not last. There remains for him another item: He must wring out the dregs — every last, bitter, poisonous remnant of sin's folly. And that taste will last to eternity.

The Christian, however, is spared the dregs. Christ has drunk them for us. He emptied for us the cup of woe, that we might drink eternally the sparkling waters of life.

That is the meaning of Lent. And as we drink the cup that our Lord gives us, we must fix our eyes on His cross. And as we do, the tasting will be blest.

PSALM 22:16, 18: *"They pierced My hands and My feet. . . . They part My garments among them and cast lots upon My vesture."*

THE NAILS AND THE DICE

Almost a thousand years before the event, the Messiah, speaking through the mouth of the psalmist, foretells His crucifixion — with all its pain, its horror, its shame. He feels the agony of the piercing nails as they tear through His flesh. Impotent, He watches the callous, jeering soldiers as they throw dice for His clothing.

We feel a sense of cold, helpless rage over the cruelty of the soldiers. We shudder at the brazen rolling of the lots. The nails and the dice — how we loathe those symbols of the Savior's death!

But we should not be too quick to blame the soldiers. We cannot view that death on the cross with detached horror.

For we are not mere spectators of that grim drama. We are participants in it. We, with all our smug respectability, with all our virtue, our piety, our pride

— we, singly and together, are to blame for the crime of Calvary.

We, who would not harm the least of God's creatures, drove the nails through the hands of God's Son. We, who would not touch a pair of dice, gambled while Love was dying.

And, to compound our guilt, we are doing it still. Every sin that we commit, every thoughtless word, every proud gesture, every impure thought, every selfish act — these are nothing less than nails that tear the Savior's flesh, rattling dice that flout His love.

The amazing lesson of Lent and Holy Week, however, is that His love still goes out — warm and saving and strong — to those who are driving the nails and who are casting the dice. Our cruelty He repays with kindness. Our scorn He rewards with grace. Our sins He removes with His blood.

To receive His pardon, to live by His power, all that we need is faith. Faith in His atoning sacrifice for our sin, faith that He lived and died as our Substitute and rose again for our justification; faith that accepts Him both as its Author and its Object.

When the Spirit implants such faith in our hearts and makes it active in love, then the hands that drove the nails and cast the dice cease from their shameful task and clasp in prayer — prayer to Him who bore the sting of death Himself that He might remove death's sting from us.

> PSALM 85:6: *"Wilt Thou not revive us again, that Thy people may rejoice in Thee?"*

AN EARLY INTIMATION
OF IMMORTALITY

The idea of immortality is an almost universal concept. Virtually every religion holds forth the idea of immortality, either as an outright promise or at least as a vague intimation.

Christianity is different. It, too, of course, teaches the immortality of the soul. But, unlike all other religions, this doctrine is centered in Christ, God's Son, our Redeemer. Through Him we look not only for the immortality of the soul, but also for the resurrection of the body. Because He rose, we, too, shall rise.

The resurrection from the dead is not simply a neat doctrinal statement that we glibly recite as a part of the Apostles' Creed. It is rather a dynamic force in our daily Christian living. It is dramatically prefigured in the Sacrament of Holy Baptism, which gives us the power each day "to walk in newness of life." It gives us the sure hope that temporal death is not the end. It conveys the guarantee of eternal fellowship with God — yes, and with all His saints, including our loved ones who have gone before.

On the basis of this immortal hope, the psalmist in our text prays: "Wilt Thou not revive us again?" There are times in life when we sink beneath the load of worry and woe and sin. Our heart almost fails us for fear and grief.

Just at such times we can echo the psalmist's plea: "Wilt Thou not revive us again?" And we can come before God with this petition because we have the firm assurance that He *will* revive us. If He will revive our bodies from the grave on the Resurrection morn, is He not both able and willing to revive our drooping spirits and lighten our heavy load? Will He not put hope in our heart and a song on our lips? He who has promised the greater — will He not perform the lesser? He will keep on reviving us all through life with the divine stimulus of His love.

Thus revived, the psalmist declares: "That Thy people may rejoice in Thee." Here is cause for rejoicing indeed. We have a God who hears our prayers, cares for our needs, lifts the heavy pack off our shoulders. He has promised that all through life He will guide us with His counsel and afterward receive us to glory.

The glimpse of that glory is enough to revive the weariest traveler along life's way. The coming of Easter proves again that the glimpse is no mirage. It is real as God is real.

This is the power of the resurrection hope. It makes us revive. It makes us rejoice.

> PSALM 85:11: *"Truth shall spring out of the earth; and righteousness shall look down from heaven."*

TRUTH'S TRIUMPHANT SPRING

Easter is more than a festival of reborn spring; more than an occasion to display the newest fashions; more even than a symbol of human hope.

Easter commemorates the resurrection of Christ. That resurrection is more than a lovely legend. It is a historical fact. Easter gives more than an intimation of immortality. Easter is the guarantee of eternal life.

Easter is true because Christ is true. He who said of Himself, "I am the Truth" also said, "I am the Resurrection and the Life." He was clear and sure in promising to arise on the third day after His death.

Easter proves again that Jesus is not merely truthful, but that He is Truth itself. On the glorious Resurrection morn that Truth sprang out of the earth.

The bonds of death could not hold Him. He burst the tomb asunder. He said "Fie!" to the hosts of hell. God would not suffer His Holy One to see corruption. Truth sprang out of the earth, as He truly had foretold.

Truth's opposite is falsehood. The devil is the father of lies. He would make us believe that death is the end of all; that Jesus stayed in the grave, after all; that Easter is a myth.

But the prince of hell has met his Master in the Lord of Life. His lies are transparent. Truth has sprung out of the earth. The hope of Easter is real.

And thus the psalmist continues: "Righteousness shall look down from heaven." Easter means that our sins lie buried in the tomb. The atoning work is done. God's righteous demands are met. We, too, shall rise to endless life.

All this Christ has done for us. All this is proved by the empty tomb. All this has made us at one with God.

Too good to be true? Ah, no — supremely good and at the same time supremely true.

For this we have no lesser guarantee than God's own Truth — that Truth which, on Easter, sprang out of the earth.

PSALM 68:11: *"The Lord gave the word; great was the company of those that published it."*

THE GREAT COMPANY

Pentecost is a glad festival. It betokens the coming of the Spirit of Truth, who leads His people into all truth. This is the Comforter whom the Savior, before He left the earth, promised to send to His disciples. This is the Paraclete who came, in wind and flame, to the assembled Christians in Jerusalem, filling the room with His presence and lighting their souls with His warmth.

And when He came upon them, they all began to speak — to speak with other tongues, "as the Spirit gave them utterance." They spoke, and men were strangely stirred. They spoke, and the Christian Church was born. The Gospel had begun its victorious, eternal course — through the nations, through the ages.

On Pentecost the psalmist's words came true: "The Lord gave the word; great was the company of those that published it." The Word came from God — the

Word of salvation and life. And the company that published it was great indeed — the mighty, countless host of the redeemed.

The Lord still gives the Word. He gives it every time the message of salvation is preached from a Christian pulpit; every time a Christian opens his Bible; every time a group of believers gather in His name to study that Word and to ponder its sacred meaning; every time a little one hears of God's love from the lips of parent or teacher; every time a child of God communes with his Lord in prayer.

But more. He gives that Word every time an infant is brought to the baptismal font, every time a Christian kneels at the altar rail to receive the blest Communion. For the Word that is spoken and taught and read is no less real and no less powerful when it comes in baptismal water or when it is clothed in bread and wine. For the written Word and the sacramental Word both reveal Him who is the Word made flesh. It is He who on Pentecost was preached to the people; to Him they were converted; in Him they were baptized; for Him the apostles witnessed; in Him the martyrs died.

Down through the centuries that Word has been proclaimed. And the great company that has published it has grown greater still with every passing age. Truly "their line is gone out through all the earth, and their words to the end of the world."

We are the heirs of the Pentecostal promise. Our hearts have been enkindled with the Pentecostal fire. May our voices ever publish the Pentecostal Word!

PSALM 119:164: *"Seven times a day do I praise Thee because of Thy righteous judgments."*

SEVEN TIMES A DAY

The annual Thanksgiving season affords the opportunity to review once again the multitude of blessings, national and personal, material and spiritual, that a gracious God has bestowed upon us. But the Christian does not wait for a presidential proclamation to bestir him to give thanks to God. Nor does he restrict his thanksgiving to the fourth Thursday of each November.

How often should we give thanks to God? "Seven times a day," says the psalmist. This is not an arbitrary figure; the psalmist is not advocating a mechanical prayer schedule, as the Moslems have. That kind of arrangement degenerates quickly into a mere outward routine.

"Seven times a day" is simply the psalmist's way of saying that he gives thanks to God at every opportunity. Every time he thinks of God, gratitude fills his heart. And, whenever possible, he gives voice to his thankful spirit.

How often do we thank God for all that He does for us? Seven times a day? Or just once a week — in church on Sunday morning? Do we thank Him just by "rattling off" our formal, familiar prayers? Or does our thanksgiving well from a dedicated heart?

Actually, when we say with the psalmist, "Seven times a day do I praise Thee," we mean that our whole life is to be an expression of thanksgiving. Our praise of God is not something that we utter; it is something that we *live*.

We have ample reason to praise God: "Because of Thy righteous judgments," as the psalmist declares. His dealings with us are always good and kind and upright. They show Him to be a God of love.

Thanksgiving Day reminds us again of the bounties without measure that have come from the hand of God: food and clothing and shelter, safety and comfort and health. Indeed, as Luther puts it, "everything that we need to support this body and life."

But we must praise Him especially for the greatest boon of all: forgiveness of sin and the hope of heaven through faith in the atoning blood of Jesus Christ. This, above all, is His "righteous judgment" — a judgment based not upon our own righteousness, but upon the righteous merits of His Son.

How often shall we praise our God? Seven times a day? No, rather "seventy times seven."

PSALM 89:3-5: *"I have made a covenant with My chosen, I have sworn unto David, My servant. Thy Seed will I establish forever and build up thy throne to all generations. And the heavens shall praise Thy wonders, O Lord."*

GOD KEEPS HIS PROMISES

On the first Christmas God kept His promise. It was a promise first given in the Garden of Eden, repeated with ever greater emphasis to the patriarchs, and voiced with increasing clarity through the prophets. This was the promise of the coming Savior, the incarnation of God's Son to redeem mankind from sin.

To David, too, mighty hero of faith and chosen servant of God, this promise was conveyed. As the psalmist here records it, God's promise took this form: "Thy Seed will I establish forever and build up thy throne to all generations." David's seed was the Messiah, born of "the house and lineage of David." We hail "the Lord's Anointed, great David's greater Son."

Through Him, David's family would be established forever. Not through a physical descent, to be sure, but through a spiritual lineage. As Christians, we in spirit belong to David's family. We are members of the royal household, and Prince Messiah is our elder Brother. His throne endures forever.

This, then, is the message of Christmas: The Lord Jesus Christ, Son of David and Son of God, has come to earth in fulfillment of the ancient prophecy. He is the Prince of Peace, whose gracious rule extends over all the sons of men as they come to lay their tribute at His feet.

This is a great and mighty wonder indeed. It is a wonder that evokes even the adoration of the heavens. "The heavens shall praise Thy wonders, O Lord," the psalmist exclaims.

On the blest Christmas night this promise was fulfilled. The vault of heaven opened and the skies were ablaze with light and the angel choir chanted the glad refrain: "Glory to God in the highest, and on earth peace, good will toward men."

Thus God kept His promise to David. Thus God keeps His promise to us. We see the heavens open. We hear the angels' song. We welcome the royal Infant and kneel at His manger-throne.

> PSALM 29:11: *"The Lord will bless His people with peace."*

PEACE FROM ABOVE

Is peace a lost art? It might almost seem so, as the spirit of intolerance and oppression continues to stalk the earth in this "cold war" era. But into our distressful, weary world comes again the spirit of the Prince of Peace to assure the children of men that peace is not a fantasy, not a delusion, not a ghost of bygone days nevermore to be recaptured; but that peace — even in this grim and anxious today — is the most real and precious treasure of the human soul.

For at Christmas we hear again the ageless song of the angels over Bethlehem's fields: "Glory to God in the highest, and on earth peace, good will toward men." And perhaps the very fact that we must again this year celebrate Christmas in a world faced with uncertainty and bent on atomic destruction will cause us to hear a bit more clearly the angels' melody of peace and to understand a bit more truly the promise of the psalmist: "The

Lord will bless His people with peace." That blessing is ours alone through Christ, the Prince of Peace.

For the peace He brought to mankind that first Christmas morning and which He has bestowed on His followers through the ages of time is not a material, earthly peace, but a spiritual, heavenly peace; not a peace for the body, but a peace for the soul; not a peace for any short and limited duration of time, but a peace that will last to all eternity; not a peace dependent upon the whims and ambitions of earthly rulers, but a peace guaranteed by the solemn pledge of a sovereign God; not a peace contracted by any earth-bound alliance, but a peace established between God and man and sealed in the blood that flowed on Calvary. That is the peace of heart and soul and conscience that assures us that we are the children of God; that peace enables us to rise above the sorrows and trials of life. That is the peace concerning which Christ Himself declared: "Peace I leave with you; My peace I give unto you."

That is the peace of which the Christmas angels sang. That is the peace of which Christ has become the Prince. That is the peace of which the psalmist spoke. That peace is the blessing of God.

And that is the peace which, in a world of tears and worry and hate, can make us strong and sure and glad.